OECD Green Growth Studies

Creating Incentives for Greener Products

A POLICY MANUAL FOR EASTERN PARTNERSHIP COUNTRIES

Please cite this publication as:
OECD (2015), *Creating Incentives for Greener Products: A Policy Manual for Eastern Partnership Countries*, OECD Green Growth Studies, OECD Publishing, Paris.
http://dx.doi.org/10.1787/9789264244542-en

ISBN 978-92-64-24453-5 (print)
ISBN 978-92-64-24454-2 (PDF)

Series: OECD Green Growth Studies
ISSN 2222-9515 (print)
ISSN 2222-9523 (online)

Photo credits: Cover © design by advitam for the OECD.

Foreword

The objective of the document is to help the European Union's Eastern Partnership (EaP) countries (Armenia, Azerbaijan, Belarus, Georgia, Moldova and Ukraine) to design or reform economic instruments related to environmentally harmful products in order to provide incentives for both reducing pollution and introducing greener products. It has been developed within the framework of the initiative "Greening Economies in the Eastern Neighbourhood" (EaP GREEN) funded by the European Commission and implemented by the OECD in partnership with the UNEP, UNIDO and UNECE. The target audience of this policy manual includes key government stakeholders (ministries of environment, economy and finance) as well as the business community, non-governmental and academic institutions in EaP countries.

This policy manual considers the potential use and implementation of four categories of product-related economic instruments: product taxes, tax differentiation based on environmental factors, deposit-refund systems and extended producer responsibility (EPR). EaP countries struggle with a number of environmental challenges that can be addressed through these instruments, including the rapid growth of the use of motor vehicles and associated emissions of carbon dioxide and local air pollutants, as well as the lack of sound waste management solutions for end-of-life vehicles and their parts; the exponential increase of municipal solid waste from packaging and electric and electronic equipment; the indiscriminate use of pesticides and fertilisers in agriculture, etc. All EaP countries are interested in expanding the use of product-related economic instruments, particularly taxes on environmentally harmful products and EPR.

This document was prepared by Dr Stephen Smith of University College London (UK) under the guidance of Eugene Mazur of the OECD Environment Directorate. In presenting multiple examples of practices in OECD countries, particularly EU Member States, it draws on the OECD work on environmentally related taxes, its Economic Instruments Database, and other literature on the design and implementation of product-related economic instruments. Past work on economic instruments of environmental policy carried out by the OECD/EAP Task Force in Eastern Europe, the Caucasus and Central Asia has also contributed to the analysis.

The authors gratefully acknowledge useful comments by Brendan Gillespie, Nils-Axel Braathen, Angela Bularga and Peter Borkey of the OECD Environment Directorate; contributions made by the European Union (EU) and the country experts of the EU's Eastern Partnership (EaP) before and during the regional expert meeting on 6-7 March 2014 in Paris; as well as the support provided by Irina Massovets and Reka Mazur.

Table of contents

Tables

Figures

Boxes

Abbreviations and Acronyms

DRS	Deposit-refund system
EaP	European Union's Eastern Partnership
ELV	End-of-life vehicle
EPR	Extended producer responsibility
EU	European Union
EUR	Euro
GDP	Gross Domestic Product
OECD	Organisation for Economic Co-operation and Development
PRO	Producer Responsibility Organisation
UNECE	United Nations Economic Commission for Europe
UNEP	United Nations Environment Programme
UNIDO	United Nations Industrial Development Organisation
VAT	Value added tax
WEEE	Waste electrical and electronic equipment

Executive summary

Promoting green growth requires well-designed institutions and environmental policy instruments that are effective in achieving their environmental objectives without imposing excessive burdens on the economy. There is growing recognition in OECD countries that economic instruments such as environmentally related taxes can be effective in stimulating a shift to less-damaging forms of production and consumption while providing producers and consumers with flexibility in making these adjustments. Behavioural changes stimulated by economic instruments may lead to the creation of new jobs and employment opportunities. Investments in new "cleaner" technology can be an important source of employment and business development. Where economic instruments generate revenues, the appropriate deployment of these revenues can also make a significant contribution to enhancing incomes and growth.

This policy manual considers the potential use and implementation of product-related economic instruments as part of a portfolio of environmental policy measures.

Product-related instruments are those which regulate the sale and use of products, rather than those directed at environmental aspects of production. Four broad categories of product-related economic instruments are discussed:

- ***Environmentally related product taxes***, levied on the sale of a product or group of products. These include taxes, such as those on motor fuels and other energy products, with an important environmental dimension, even if the principal purpose of the tax is revenue generation.
- ***Tax differentiation***, under which existing revenue-raising taxes are adapted to reflect environmental objectives, increasing the rates of tax on "dirty" goods and/or reducing the rates of tax on "green" goods to achieve behavioural changes in production or consumption.
- ***Deposit-refund systems (DRS)***, which are used to recover product packaging, drinks containers, or end-of-life products, especially those which would be hazardous or toxic within the general waste stream.
- ***Extended Producer Responsibility (EPR)***, under which various obligations are imposed on producers, either individually or collectively, e.g. to recover and recycle end-of-life products.

A crucial early step in developing policy towards product-based economic instruments is selecting instruments which are appropriate to the relevant environmental problems and policy objectives, and which are capable of achieving the required environmental improvements. The various product-based economic instruments covered in this document all have strengths and weaknesses which make them suitable for use in certain contexts and applications and less effective, or more costly or burdensome to the economy, in others. Much greater impact is likely to be achieved if a small number of products are targeted by carefully designed instruments than if product-based instruments are applied to a large number of products.

The experience of OECD countries suggests that the use of some product-based economic instruments has been more successful than others, and that there may be potential to successfully apply economic instruments beyond the products covered by OECD experience. However, the pattern of OECD experience reflects some underlying strengths and weaknesses of these instruments, which have meant that the majority of the applications lie in a relatively small number of fields:

- Taxes on ***motor fuels, other energy products, and on motor vehicles***. Together these account for well over 90% of all revenue from environmentally related taxes in OECD countries.
- Taxes, deposit-refund systems and EPR applying to ***packaging products and materials***;
- Taxes, deposit-refund systems and EPR applying to ***products liable to generate hazardous wastes***, such as batteries, used motor oils, pesticides, fertilisers and certain electrical and electronic goods.

Within the broad pattern of existing applications of product-based economic instruments, it can be seen that the instruments fall into two broad groups:

1. ***Instruments directed at achieving behavioural changes in consumer purchasing behaviour.*** Taxes on the sale of products have their main effects through changes in consumer purchasing behaviour and in the supply of products by firms. The higher tax will increase the price of "dirty" goods to consumers, and reduce the profitability of producers of these goods, encouraging both to shift to cleaner alternatives.
2. ***Instruments directed at achieving changes in waste generation and waste management.*** Taxes can be used to discourage the sale of certain products that involve high costs of end-of-life waste management – such as polluting batteries – and to encourage consumers to switch to alternatives (such as rechargeable batteries). However, deposit-refund systems and EPR can be targeted more precisely to achieve separation of wastes so as to promote greater re-use, recycling or the safer waste management of particularly hazardous materials.

The policy manual lays out the key principles that will help to ensure the environmental effectiveness of these instruments, addresses main design issues and legal and institutional arrangements for their implementation.

1. Strategic approach to using product-related economic instruments

This policy manual considers the potential use and implementation of four categories of product-related economic instruments: product taxes, tax differentiation based on environmental factors, deposit-refund systems and extended producer responsibility (EPR). Each of these instruments has particular strengths and weaknesses that make them appropriate with respect to certain policies and products, but may reduce their applicability elsewhere. This section proposes an approach to identify instruments which are appropriate for the particular environmental problem under consideration.

1.1 Types of instruments

This policy manual considers the potential use and implementation of product-related economic instruments as part of a portfolio of environmental policy measures. Product-related instruments are those which regulate the sale and use of products, rather than those directed at environmental aspects of the production process. Four broad categories of product-related economic instruments can be distinguished:

- ***Product taxes:*** These include taxes levied on the sale of a product or group of products with an important environmental dimension to either production or consumption. This category includes both those taxes which have been explicitly introduced for environmental reasons and the much broader group of taxes, such as those on motor fuels and other energy products, which have significant environmental implications, even if the principal purpose of the tax is revenue generation. Regardless of the original motivation of the tax, it can have environmental effects through its influence on the behaviour of producers and consumers. Some other environmentally related product taxes have been introduced with the intention to provide a source of earmarked revenues for environmental purposes (e.g. to contribute revenues to an environmental clean-up fund).
- ***Tax differentiation based on environmental factors:*** The structure of existing revenue-raising taxes may be adapted to reflect environmental objectives, increasing the rates of tax on "dirty" goods and/or reducing the rates of tax on "green" goods. Generally the aim of this is to achieve behavioural changes, in the form of a shift of production or consumption away from dirty goods towards cleaner ones. Tax differentiation usually takes the form of a broadly revenue-neutral package of tax changes, with increases in some tax rates and reductions in others, so the overall effect on revenue is rather small.
- ***Deposit-refund systems (DRS):*** DRS are commonly used to ensure high rates of recovery for certain specific items that can be re-used or recycled (e.g. drinks containers), or to encourage return of end-of-life products or materials that would otherwise be dangerous or too costly to dispose of as part of the general waste stream. A charge is levied when the product is sold and then fully or partly refunded when the good or its container are returned after use. Such arrangements can be mandatory or instituted on an entirely voluntary basis by producers themselves, where the recovery of items is sufficiently valuable (e.g. reusable printer cartridges).
- ***Extended producer responsibility (EPR):*** EPR is defined by OECD (2001) as "the idea that producers should be made physically or financially liable for the social costs of disposal (including the environmental impact) at the end of the product life". Superficially very different from the first three groups of product-based economic instruments, EPR schemes typically take the form of legislation imposing various obligations on producers, including rules requiring them to recover and recycle end-of-life products. Producers – either individually or collectively – may comply with these obligations by setting up arrangements to encourage a high rate of product return and recycling.

1.2 Clarifying policy objectives

The first step in the development of any policy instrument should be to establish the underlying policy objectives. What is the purpose of introducing the instrument? Only when this is clarified can key questions be asked, about whether the instrument is capable of achieving the intended objectives, whether there might be better alternatives, and so on.

Behavioural change

A significant reason for environmental policy-makers to consider any of the four potential instruments discussed in this manual is their potential to stimulate changes in the behaviour of producers or consumers that reduce polluting emissions or other damage to the environment.

In the case of ***product taxes and environmental tax differentiation*** this is achieved through the effects on the pricing of products and the profits of firms. If the product tax is passed forward to consumers in higher product prices, and if it is levied at a sufficiently high rate, then consumers will be incentivised to reduce their consumption of dirty goods and to switch to cleaner, untaxed alternatives. If producers cannot pass the tax forward to customers in higher prices, the effect of the tax will be felt in reduced profitability, and this will encourage firms to switch to producing untaxed alternatives. Either way, the incentive effect of the tax steers decisions towards cleaner outcomes.

In the case of ***deposit-refund systems***, the principal behavioural change comes through the incentive that the refund of the initial deposit gives for returning the used product or container. If the amount refunded per bottle is sufficiently high, consumers will go to the trouble of bringing their bottles back for refund, and even those bottles that are discarded may be collected and returned by scavengers, enticed by the money that can be earned from the refund.

An important part of the behavioural effect is that it achieves separate recovery of different materials or products, as opposed to the undifferentiated recovery of mixed wastes in the general waste stream, and this separation has two main motivations. In some cases (e.g. batteries) the aim is to ensure secure and safe collection and disposal of substances or products that would otherwise be hazardous or harmful within the general waste stream. In other cases (traditionally, bottles), deposit-refund arrangements ensure separate collection of substances or products to permit cost-effective re-use, recycling or materials recovery.

In addition to the behavioural incentive for recovery, a deposit-refund system may affect initial purchasing behaviour. The initial deposit acts like a product tax on those consumers who do not intend to return the product and redeem the deposit. If, in addition, the operating costs of the system are significant, the price of products subject to deposit-refund arrangements may rise, which may discourage their purchase or production. This is the reason why many of the deposit-refund systems for bottles and other drinks containers that were previously operated by drinks manufacturers on a voluntary basis have died out in recent decades, as they have been undermined by competition from suppliers selling "single-use" disposable containers (e.g. beer in cans rather than bottles).

With ***extended producer responsibility (EPR)***, a range of behavioural changes are possible, and may be stimulated depending on how the scheme is designed. Producers may, for example, be motivated to set up efficient systems for recovery, consumers may be encouraged to return products through these systems, and so on. In addition, some EPR schemes aim to incentivise waste-reducing product innovation directed at achieving a shift towards the production and sale of "greener" products, with lower end-of-life disposal costs – so-called "design-for-environment" (DFE) innovation. In principle, when producers are responsible for these costs, they have a reason to take them into account in product design and manufacture. However, as discussed later, setting up an EPR scheme so that it has the potential to achieve DFE innovation requires the scheme to be designed in a particular way, and may not always be achievable.

As with costly deposit-refund systems, EPR may also affect the prices at which goods are sold – perhaps quite significantly, if the obligations imposed on firms are costly to achieve. This may affect production and consumption behaviour in a way very similar to the imposition of a significant product tax.

Many of these behavioural effects will be governed by the decisions made about policy parameters, such as the rate at which a product tax is levied, or the required recovery rate under EPR. A higher product tax will naturally discourage dirty consumption more than a small tax. Likewise, requiring firms to achieve a very high rate of recovery under EPR may impose significantly higher costs on them, that will either adversely affect their profitability and competitiveness or will be passed on to consumers in significantly higher prices, leading to larger behavioural changes in the product market.

Effect on tax revenues

A second significant motivation for the use of some product-related economic instruments may be the revenues that could be generated. In particular, a product tax or charge would generate revenues which could be used for some particular purpose (e.g. an environmental fund) or as an additional contribution to the general public budget.

Tax differentiation could be implemented in a way that increases public revenues by increasing the rates of tax on "dirty" goods while leaving other tax rates largely unchanged. However, tax differentiation could also take the form of selective reductions in the rates of tax on "green" goods such as insulation materials or recycled products, and if no offsetting increases were made to tax rates on other goods, the revenue effect would be negative. A revenue-neutral reform would also be possible, which would combine tax increases on some dirty goods, together with tax reductions on some green goods, to leave overall tax revenues – and hence the tax burden – unchanged.

Revenue considerations are rarely a motivation for the introduction of deposit refund systems or EPR. Deposit-refund systems typically raise revenues through the initial deposit, but this money is then partly or wholly refunded at a later date. Extended producer responsibility has little revenue-raising potential, although in some applications EPR has been combined with the introduction of a tax or charge to finance the system of product recovery and recycling.

Impact on public budgets

The impact of product-based economic instruments on public budgets may be a significant consideration. This is likely to be most significant in the case of instruments directed at waste management. Both deposit-refund systems and EPR are intended to divert significant waste flows from the publicly-financed general waste stream, so that savings will be made on municipal waste collection and disposal. Indeed, one of the factors that may have made EPR particularly attractive to policy-makers is that it holds out the prospect of achieving higher rates of recycling while at the same time reducing the financial burden of publicly-financed waste management operations.

1.3 Wider implications of instrument choices

Policy decisions to employ product-related economic instruments need to achieve these positive objectives while at the same time having regard to a range of possible consequences, some of which may be less desirable.

Effects on public administration

The resources required to administer and enforce product taxes and charges may be large relative to the revenues generated, leaving little or no net revenue generated after the additional operating costs are deducted. This is likely to be a particular issue with tax differentiation, which may raise little revenue (if some tax rates are reduced while others are increased), but which may significantly add to the complexity of tax administration, and hence to its cost.

Evidence on the scale of administrative costs associated with environmentally related product taxes is sparse. For example, while Denmark has a number of well documented "green" taxes on energy products, environmentally harmful products and on motor vehicles, but it is impossible to calculate their administrative costs separately from those of other taxes operated by the Danish Ministry of Taxation. However, the operating costs of environmentally related product taxes seem likely to be broadly proportionate to the number of firms that are subject to each tax: the more firms are involved, the higher the administrative burden. One practical implication, noted by Pavel and Vítek (2012) and by Hogg et al (2014), is that environmentally related product taxes should be levied as far back in the production chain as possible so that relatively few firms are involved. A good example of this is the mineral oil excise, which requires intensive monitoring due to its very high rates, but which involves only a limited number of large-scale importers and refiners.

Effects on businesses

Costs borne by the regulated firms will include the counterparts of the public sector's administrative and enforcement costs: a significant part of any system of taxation is borne by taxpayers, who have to fill in tax returns, keep records, deal with correspondence and enforcement audits, etc. A further source of costs to regulated firms is likely to arise where deposit-refund systems or EPR are employed as the policy instrument. Under these instruments, a large part of the burden of operating the waste collection and disposal system is shifted to firms.

Where regulated firms face international competitors who are not subject to the same regulation (either importers or competitors in export markets overseas), the use of product-based economic instruments may have adverse effects on the ***competitiveness*** of national firms *vis-à-vis* these competitors. In general, it is desirable for imported goods to be subject to any environmentally related product taxes, deposit-refund systems or EPR obligations on the same basis as domestic production. Applying these instruments equally to domestic production and imported goods will also ensure that environmental policy does not become used as indirect trade protection, reducing consumer choices and weakening the incentives for domestic production efficiency.

Product-related economic instruments can also create ***business opportunities*** in two main areas. First, as consumers switch away from the taxed "dirty" products, the market for cleaner alternatives will expand. Such effects are likely in most cases to be relatively small and gradual, but nonetheless are a positive counterpart to the loss of sales that would be suffered by firms producing the taxed "dirty" products. The timing and predictability of the introduction of environmentally related tax measures affect the extent to which domestic firms can benefit from the opportunities offered by this switch in consumer purchasing and the extent to which the additional demand for cleaner alternative products is met instead by additional imports. A phased introduction with sufficient advance warning of the tax measure will give domestic firms a chance to invest in capacity to meet the new consumer demand. By contrast, an abrupt introduction of large tax incentives, especially in a context where there is doubt that they will be sustained over time, will tend to mean that the new consumer demand is met by imports.

A second area where new business opportunities arise is when product-based instruments are used to achieve changes in waste management. DRS and EPR create business opportunities in waste management and recycling, especially for firms offering waste collection and processing services, and for producers and users of recycled materials. Again, careful planning and publicity about the changes being made increases the possibility that domestic firms are in a position to take advantage of the new opportunities that arise.

Effects on consumers

One of the main channels through which product-based economic instruments can influence the purchasing behaviour of consumers and the production decisions of firms is the impact that they have on product prices. An additional tax on the sale of a commodity is likely to be passed forward, to some extent, to consumers through higher product prices. The extent to which this happens will be governed by market conditions in the product market concerned. For example, where sales of the product are highly responsive to increases in the product price (where demand is "price elastic"), rather less of the tax will be passed forward to consumers, and rather more will remain with the seller in terms of reduced profits or be passed back to employees in lower wages. By contrast, where the market for the taxed product is not particularly price-sensitive (where demand is "price-inelastic") rather more of the tax will be passed to consumers in higher prices. These effects are governed by the characteristics of the market, and cannot be over-ridden by legislative provisions or the mechanism through which the tax is levied.

In addition to the extra tax burden, product-based instruments affect consumers in other ways. In particular, if the instrument induces consumers to change their behaviour, consumers may bear additional costs or inconvenience. For example, product-based instruments that induce consumers to separate wastes and return different wastes to appropriate collection points (bottle banks, etc.) will require consumers to spend time and effort in waste separation, and time and possibly money (for motor fuel, etc.) in separately returning different products. While these effects may be small for most consumers, they may nonetheless be significant when added over all consumers.

A further area of concern about effects on consumers is the possibility that the additional tax burden, and possibly other costs, may be a particularly heavy burden on poorer households. This may be most significant where product-based instruments are applied to "necessity" goods such as domestic energy which form a relatively high proportion of the spending of poorer households.

Effects on prices and inflation

All the policy instruments discussed in this manual would be expected to increase, to some extent at least, the price of environmentally damaging products. Indeed, this effect is part of the mechanism by which instruments such as product taxes and EPR enhance environmental sustainability through changes in producer and consumer behaviour. However, policy reforms which increase prices are likely to raise concerns about their possible impact on inflation. This can be a matter of considerable political sensitivity at a time of wider economic change, and this aspect will need to be taken into account in the design and introduction of market incentives for greener products. For example, measures to increase the taxation on motor fuels and other energy products may be desirable from an environmental point of view, but need careful timing, as it will be difficult to justify significant increases in energy taxes at a time when world energy prices are rising sharply.

Nevertheless, the potential inflationary impact of environmental product taxes and EPR should not be exaggerated. With the exception of taxes on motor vehicles and motor fuels, the instruments discussed in this manual would have rather small one-off effects on prices. EPR may increase product prices, but at the same time reduce the burden of local taxes needed to finance municipal waste management. Some taxes may indeed raise prices, but the revenues collected would allow other taxes to be correspondingly reduced. This can be demonstrated most clearly by environmental product tax differentiation, which simultaneously increases the price of some products while reducing the price of others, with negligible impact on the overall price level.

Effects on overall functioning of the market economy

A market economy operates efficiently when there is competition between firms, and when any necessary environmental or other regulation is proportionate, well-targeted, and does not unnecessarily inhibit processes of market competition and innovation. One of the great attractions of economic instruments in environmental policy is that they can guide consumers and producers to take account of the environmental consequences of production and consumption without imposing unnecessarily costly rigid and bureaucratic regulation. Producers and consumers are incentivised to improve the environment, but have the flexibility to do this in ways that are less costly, and can avoid excessively costly options. The design of product-related economic instruments needs to ensure that, as far as practicable, it achieves the desired environmental effects, while permitting the maximum flexibility as to how this outcome is achieved, and avoiding features that would damage normal processes of market functioning, competition and innovation.

1.4 Choice of instruments

A crucial early step in developing policy towards product-based economic instruments is selecting instruments which are ***appropriate*** to the relevant environmental problems and policy objectives, and which are ***capable*** of achieving the required environmental improvements. The available instruments - environmental product taxes and tax differentiation, deposit-refund systems and EPR – all have strengths and weaknesses, which make them suitable for use in certain contexts and applications, and less effective, or more costly or burdensome to the economy, in others. Much greater impact is likely to be achieved if a small number of products are targeted by carefully designed instruments, than if product-based instruments are applied indiscriminately to a large number of products without careful design and targeting.

The experience of OECD countries, analysed in Chapter 2, indicates the range of products where product-based economic instruments have been applied. Some applications have been more successful than others, and there may be potential for successful applications that go beyond the products covered by OECD experience. However, the pattern of OECD experience does reflect some underlying strengths and weaknesses of these instruments, which have meant that the majority of the applications lie in a relatively small number of fields:

- Taxes, deposit-refund systems and EPR applying to motor vehicles;
- Taxes on energy products, including motor fuels and household energy;
- Taxes on pesticides and fertilisers;
- Taxes, deposit-refund systems and EPR applying to packaging products and materials; and
- Taxes, deposit-refund systems and EPR applying to products liable to generate hazardous wastes, such as batteries, used motor oils, and certain electrical and electronic goods.

These various applications of product-based economic instruments are all in areas where the instruments are capable, to a greater or lesser extent, of achieving behavioural changes with desirable environmental consequences. For example, a significant part of the rationale for high taxes on motor fuels and household energy is that these should stimulate consumers to save energy, for example by choosing smaller, more fuel-efficient vehicles, or by making more journeys by public transport. Similarly, EPR policies in the area of product packaging are intended to discourage excessive packaging, by making producers liable to bear the waste management costs for product packaging. Selecting and designing product-based economic instruments needs to start with a clear appraisal of the environmental goals of the policy, and the changes in behaviour that will be needed to meet these goals. Instruments then need to be identified that have the potential to achieve the desired changes in behaviour.

Within the broad pattern of existing applications of product-based economic instruments, it can be seen that the instruments fall into two broad groups:

- Instruments aimed at changing consumers' purchasing behaviour; and
- Instruments directed at achieving changes in waste generation and waste management.

Taxes on the sale of products have their main effects through changes in consumer purchasing behaviour and in the supply of products by firms. There are a range of different possible existing and new product taxes that could be used for environmental policy purposes. These include existing general sales taxes (such as value added tax), excise taxes levied on motor fuels and other specific commodities, customs duties and other taxes charged on imported goods, and possible new taxes introduced on particular commodities or activities. With existing taxes it should be possible to increase the rate of tax on environmentally-damaging goods or reduce the tax on "clean" goods that benefit the environment (e.g. energy-saving products, public transport, etc.).

Taxes on the sale of certain products may also be used to reduce waste management costs when waste packaging or end-of-life products are discarded. High taxes can be used to discourage the sale of certain products that involve high costs of end-of-life waste management – such as polluting batteries – and to encourage consumers to switch to alternatives (such as rechargeable batteries). However, two of the available instruments – deposit-refund systems and EPR – can be targeted more precisely at aspects of waste management that cannot easily be addressed through taxes levied at the point when products are sold. Both DRS and EPR can, in particular, be used to achieve the separation of wastes so as to promote greater re-use and recycling or the safer waste management of particularly hazardous materials.

Deposit-refund systems are typically applied to ensure high rates of recovery of certain tightly defined and specific products, where the mechanism of charging deposits and paying refunds can be operated at acceptable cost, relative to the gains from achieving high rates of return of the products concerned. First, there are those, such as drinks bottles or cans, where significant savings in raw materials or environmental costs can be achieved through a waste management system that ensures a high rate of return and recycling. Second, there are products where it would be costly or hazardous if wastes are mixed in with general household waste, such as batteries and consumer electronic goods containing toxic materials. Refunding the deposit provides an incentive that ensures a high rate of compliance with special waste treatment arrangements. EPR schemes can also be applied to achieve both of these waste management objectives. Typically, EPR schemes are much less prescriptive about how the waste management outcomes are to be achieved and place the responsibility on the participating firms to achieve the required outcome. This flexibility allows firms to select the most cost-effective ways of achieving the required outcomes. In general, EPR will be more suitable than mandatory deposit-refund systems for managing wastes from products where refund arrangements would be costly or difficult to operate.

In considering the potential scope for applying product-based economic instruments, the limits to the effectiveness and cost-efficiency of these instruments need to be understood. Product taxes are, for example, likely to be an effective way of stimulating behavioural change in consumer purchasing behaviour without excessive regulatory interference with the efficient functioning of the market economy, but cannot guarantee the scale of the behavioural response that will be achieved. This will depend on the individual decisions of consumers, faced with a higher price for the environmentally damaging product than its alternatives.

When it is crucial that policy should guarantee a particular environmental outcome, alternative regulatory approaches may be better. For example, taxes are unlikely to be a good choice where the aim is to discourage the use of hazardous products such as asbestos, and in these cases an outright regulatory ban might be more appropriate.

Table 1.1. summarises the key areas of potential application for the four types of product-based economic instruments covered in this manual.

Table 1.1. Areas of potential application of product-based economic instruments

	New product taxes	Differentiation of existing taxes	Deposit-refund systems	Extended producer responsibility
Motor vehicles	Taxation on initial sale can be used to encourage purchase of smaller, more fuel-efficient vehicles or to stimulate purchase of vehicles with particular desired characteristics. Annual vehicle use taxes are less effective in influencing consumer purchases. New sales taxes on vehicles are unlikely to be needed if substantial taxes are already levied on vehicle sales, as these can be differentiated.	Taxes levied on the sale of vehicles can be modified to reflect environmental and safety characteristics of vehicles. Annual vehicle use taxes can also be modified to reflect such characteristics, but are less effective, as they can only influence vehicle stock by accelerating scrapping of highly-polluting vehicles.	Worth considering only if unauthorised dumping of motor vehicles is a major environmental problem. Operation of the system may be complex. Risk of refunds paid on cars when no deposit was originally paid (e.g. imported used vehicles).	Making vehicle producers/importers responsible for the costs of recovery and waste management for end-of-life vehicles can stimulate well-managed collection of used vehicles and higher levels of recycling of materials/components. Rules requiring high rates of recycling of materials and components can impose significant costs on producers, and correspondingly raise vehicle prices.
Motor fuels	No need to institute new taxes on motor fuels. Existing excise taxes can be increased and/or adapted to meet environmental objectives.	A lower tax on "greener" fuels can be used to offset higher production costs of these fuels or to encourage consumers to switch fuels.	No relevant application.	No relevant application.
Motor engine oil, lubricating oils and greases	Taxes will not lead to any change in unauthorised discharge of waste oils into watercourses and public sewers – the principal environmental concern.	Not effective in reducing unauthorised discharge of waste oils.	DRS can be used to ensure collected used oil is returned to an authorised collector for safe processing.	Producers/importers could be required to ensure safe recovery and processing of used oil, but oil users need additional incentives to collect and return it.
Electricity and gas supply, and oil-based fuels for heating and other non-motor uses	Could encourage fuel saving by households and other users, although of household energy raises significant distributional issues.	Where these fuels are already taxed, there may be scope to differentiate the taxes to tax more heavily the most-polluting forms of energy.	No relevant application.	Household fuel suppliers could be required to improve the energy efficiency of their customers' household appliances, home insulation, etc.
Bottles, cans and other drinks packaging	A tax per new can or bottle can be used to encourage systems in which bottles are re-used and to discourage single-use drinks containers.	Existing sales taxes such as VAT cannot easily be differentiated so that a tax is applied per new can or bottle.	Help sustain the use of re-fillable bottles by drinks manufacturers; achieve high rates of return/recycling of single-use cans and bottles.	Could require drinks producers and/or retailers to achieve high collection rates for single-use containers.
Plastic shopping bags	A tax could be levied on the use of disposable plastic carrier bags by retailers.	There is no obvious mechanism for differentiating existing sales taxes to achieve higher rates of re-use of plastic shopping bags.	No relevant application. It would be too costly to pay refunds on such small, low-value items.	Could require retailers to limit their use of disposable carrier bags and/or to charge customers for each bag used, rather than providing bags for free.

	New product taxes	Differentiation of existing taxes	Deposit-refund systems	Extended producer responsibility
Other packaging and packaging materials	Taxes on the supply of packaging material to firms could discourage excessive packaging use and encourage innovation in re-usable packaging.	Tax rates should reflect waste management costs, with higher tax rates on sales of composite materials which cannot easily be recycled.	No relevant application due to the diversity of materials and the small quantities recovered from each consumer.	May require producers to recover and recycle used packaging.
Batteries	A tax on the sale of batteries by retailers. Alternatively, producers and importers could be taxed on the volume of their deliveries to domestic retailers.	A higher rate of VAT could be charged on the most polluting batteries, but would be difficult to administer.	Use to achieve return and safe disposal of batteries.	May oblige battery producers or retailers to create a system for safe collection and disposal of batteries (either all or most dangerous types).
Disposable products (cameras, razors, etc.)	Could be levied on the sale of disposable products by retailers or at wholesale/import stage.	Increased rate of VAT could be charged on these products.	No practicable scope for DRS.	EPR likely to be disproportionately costly.
Pesticides and other agricultural chemicals	Could be levied on sale by retailers or at the wholesale/import stage	Increased rate of VAT could be charged on these products.	Not applicable	Not applicable
Electronic equipment, electric appliances, other durable household goods	Could be levied on sale by retailers or at the wholesale/import stage	Increased rate of VAT could be charged on these products.	Consider only if dumping is a big problem or if dangerous materials require safe recovery.	Could be used to recover used refrigerants or other dangerous materials.
Car tyres	Could be levied on sale by retailers or at the wholesale/import stage.	Increased rate of VAT could be charged on tyres.	Clear incentives for tyres to be returned safely and not dumped.	Require producers and importers to operate systems for recovery, recycling of used tyres.

The choice of policy instrument is most complex where issues of waste management are the concern of policy. In these cases, product taxes, deposit-refund systems and EPR have very different advantages and disadvantages, and these are likely to balance out differently in relation to different products. Table 1.2. summarises how each of these three instruments performs in relation to the considerations discussed in Sections 1.1 and 1.2: environmental effectiveness, the impact on public revenues and costs, effects on consumer behaviour, and the burdens placed on producers and consumers.

For example, for products whose main environmental issues relate to disposal, the most appropriate product-based instruments will be those directed at disposal behaviour – DRS and EPR. Both systems typically involve the collection of products or materials that would otherwise end up in the general waste stream in order to ensure safer waste management or more effective re-use or recycling. The choice between the two is a matter of balancing effectiveness and flexibility. On the one hand, EPR can be applied to more broadly-defined elements of the waste stream, such as "packaging" or "waste electrical and electronic equipment", and it is usually implemented in a way which leaves producers more flexibility in how they meet their obligations (but requires more rigorous monitoring of compliance). On the other hand, DRS can be a straightforward way of achieving many of the aims of EPR, and many EPR schemes in international practice are implemented using DRS arrangements.

Table 1.2. Alternative economic instruments to promote waste recovery and recycling

	Product charge or tax	Deposit-refund system	Extended Producer Responsibility
Effect on recovery and recycling rates	Small or zero. Consumers pay the tax but have no reason to change disposal behaviour.	Potentially large, if refund is large enough to incentivise return. Outcome will depend on consumer responses.	If policy is properly enforced, it should achieve the required recovery target (but at unpredictable cost to firms).
Effect on public revenues	High	Nil if deposit and refund are equal.	Nil
Impact on costs of public waste management	Largely unchanged, as waste flows unaffected.	Waste volumes and costs reduced due to items returned through deposit-refund system.	Waste volumes and costs reduced due to diversion of waste to producer-run collection.
Effects on consumer behaviour	High incentive to switch to untaxed products (e.g. cans instead of taxed bottles).	Low incentive to switch to other products (unless operating costs lead firms to raise prices). Consumers who return items face zero cost (apart from inconvenience).	Depends on how EPR achieves required recovery. If producers face high costs of operating EPR, prices may have to rise.
Cost burden on producers	Loss of sales due to switching.	Significant burden of charging deposit, making refunds and storage/return costs.	Potentially high, especially if legislation sets unrealistically-high target for recovery.
Burden on consumers	Additional tax	Less additional financial burden than with product tax (due to refunds), but inconvenience costs of returning items.	High, if costs of operating EPR force producers to increase prices. Possible inconvenience costs to consumers, depending on how scheme operates.

In some cases, it may be appropriate to combine instruments: for example, to introduce a tax on packaging materials at the same time as legislation establishing EPR for packaging waste. EPR for packaging waste often takes the form of an industry-financed collection scheme for packaging waste. Industry as a whole would bear the costs of managing wastes from excessive packaging, but each individual firm would bear only a small proportion of the costs of its own packaging. EPR would give only a rather weak incentive for firms to cut down on their own packaging, and a second instrument might usefully be employed to discourage excessive packaging. A tax on packaging materials, combined with EPR, would strengthen the incentive to reduce packaging waste, and thus enhance the effect of EPR.

The effectiveness of EPR in achieving desirable changes in waste management could be further enhanced by the use of other ***complementary instruments***, which act directly on key aspects of producer or consumer behaviour. A number of EU countries use landfill taxes which, in combination with EPR, ensure that producers face the full social cost of any landfill disposal of their products, and not just the landfill operator's fees. Another complementary instrument is charges based on the weight or volume of waste that households put out for collection (so-called pay-as-you-throw charges). Charging for household waste collection based on weight or volume rather than through general municipal taxation can sharpen the incentives for household waste reduction, though care needs to be taken that such charges do not induce a rise in illegal waste disposal.

1.5 Interaction with other policy instruments

Subsidies

In OECD countries it is increasingly recognised that production and consumption in several priority areas of environmental policy are heavily distorted by environmentally harmful subsidies. Such subsidies act as "negative taxes", encouraging the production and consumption of products that have adverse environmental effects, at the same time as environmentally related taxes try to discourage this behaviour. The net effect is wasteful: the huge amount of public policy effort expended in developing new environmental policy instruments is undermined by subsidies which pull in the opposite direction.

This is particularly true of fossil fuel production and consumption, some aspects of which, such as coal mining, can be heavily subsidized, while at the same time countries are concerned about the contribution of energy sector emissions to climate change and other major environmental problems.

A substantial proportion of the support for fossil fuel production and consumption in OECD countries does not take the form of explicit financial subsidy schemes, but is delivered through less-transparent mechanisms such as tax concessions. Recent OECD work (OECD, 2012) has found that "tax expenditures" (subsidies given in the form of tax breaks and concessions) account for two thirds of the 550 reported measures that support consumption or production of fossil fuels in 34 OECD countries. Subsidies paid in the form of tax breaks are less conspicuous and may, therefore, escape the attention of legislators and the public. Nevertheless, every dollar foregone in tax revenues through tax breaks has the same cost to the public sector as a dollar spent in explicit subsidy expenditure.

Recognising this, many countries have come to see the removal of unjustified and environmentally damaging subsidies and tax breaks as a necessary prelude to the development of meaningful environmental taxes and regulation. The first step would then be the removal of environmentally harmful subsidies. The second would be the reform of existing energy taxes, to reflect more accurately the environmental aspects of production and consumption. New product-related instruments would then constitute a third step, which would be worth taking only once the potential for reform of existing subsidies and taxes has been fully exploited.

Product standards

Product standards can be used to influence the environmental consequences of consumption, by requiring products that are sold to meet requirements that would reduce their environmental impact. Examples of product standards range from car specifications to the content of harmful chemicals in consumer products.

Product standards can perform a complementary role, enhancing the impact of product taxes which are designed to steer demand to less-damaging alternatives. Thus, for example, product standards that require producers to offer less environmentally damaging products within their product range can offer consumers a greater choice, and tax incentives may then be used to steer consumers towards the less damaging option. (Thus, for example, regulatory standards on the average fuel efficiency of motor vehicles have been used in some countries to stimulate the availability of smaller and more fuel-efficient vehicles.) This combination of taxes and product regulation may be preferable to a blanket ban on the more damaging options, which can be unduly inflexible, and may deny consumers products which, for a variety of reasons, they may value strongly.

Equally, taxes can be used to enhance the impact of product standards, accelerating the pace or increasing the scale of consumer take-up of less-damaging products. For example, during the phase-out of leaded petrol in EU countries, a tax differential in favour of unleaded petrol was used to encourage motorists to switch to unleaded fuel. Again, this combination of instruments offered greater flexibility than an immediate outright ban on leaded petrol, while encouraging more rapid consumer adjustment.

Eco-labelling

Labelling of products can enhance the impact of environmentally-related tax differentiation, especially where consumers are environmentally motivated, by encouraging a shift to less-damaging products. The labelling can signal which products benefit from a tax advantage, which may help consumers understand the reasons for any difference in price. Where consumers have strong environmental motivation, taxation plus eco-labelling may be more effective in encouraging consumer substitution than taxation alone. In some countries, policy-makers have been very interested in the potential for labelling to "nudge" consumers to making "greener" consumption choices and to alter purchasing behaviour where it may not happen if consumers are simply faced with a small price differential.

Labelling of certain products can also enhance the effects of arrangements designed to improve waste management, especially those, such as EPR, that require waste separation and product return by consumers. Some products – particularly plastics – with very different waste management costs are difficult to distinguish on the basis of visual inspection, and labelling can help consumers to choose products that they can later recycle easily and to avoid products for which end-of-life disposal will be difficult or more costly.

References

OECD (2012), *Inventory of estimated budgetary support and tax expenditures for fossil fuels 2013*, OECD Publishing, Paris, http://dx.doi.org/10.1787/9789264187610-en.

OECD (2001), *Extended producer responsibility: A guidance manual for governments*, OECD Publishing, Paris, http://dx.doi.org/10.1787/9789264189867-en.

2. Lessons learned from the application of product-related economic instruments

This section provides an overview of the existing practices in OECD and EaP countries in the implementation of the four categories of product-related economic instruments. It considers the application of each instrument to various product types, its design and impact on public revenue.

2.1 Environmentally related product taxes and tax differentiation

2.1.1 Revenue-generating potential

The level and pattern of revenues from environmentally related product taxes in OECD countries illustrates the revenue-generating potential of these taxes and gives a useful indication of the most significant areas of their application.

Across the OECD area as a whole, environmentally-related taxes contribute on average almost 6% of the total tax revenues (Figure 2.1.). The average amount collected in environmentally-related taxes is of the order of USD 550 per head of population, equivalent to some 1.65% of GDP in 2010.

While environmentally-related taxes contribute substantial revenues in most OECD countries, it is clear that the contribution is dominated by taxes on only two groups of products: energy products and motor vehicles (Figure 2.2.).

- Taxes on energy products contribute about two thirds of the revenue from environmentally related taxes in OECD countries. This contribution has, however, declined over the past two decades, from revenues equivalent to about 1.4% of GDP in the early 1990s to about 1.2% by 2010 despite the growing awareness of major environmental problems arising from energy consumption. A factor in this decline is almost certainly the steep rise in world oil prices and, consequently, in the pre-tax price of motor fuels, as shown in Figure 2.2. Rising motor fuel prices have discouraged some governments from raising motor fuel taxes in line with general inflation and, as a result, the real value of these taxes has been gradually eroded.
- Taxes on motor vehicles and transport constitute a further 30% of the total revenue from environmentally related taxes. Despite the great expansion of vehicle ownership and individual travel in recent years, this revenue contribution remained broadly static through the 1990s and 2000s.
- Barely 5% of the revenues is brought in by other environmentally-related taxes. Some of these are taxes levied directly on emissions from industrial activity or the consumption of environmental services (e.g. landfill taxes). The revenue contribution made by environmentally related taxes on products other than energy and motor vehicles is very small indeed, although, as documented below, some individual countries have implemented innovative policies using carefully targeted small-scale product taxes to address environmental objectives.

Figure 2.1. Revenue from environmentally related taxes as a percentage of total tax revenue in selected OECD countries

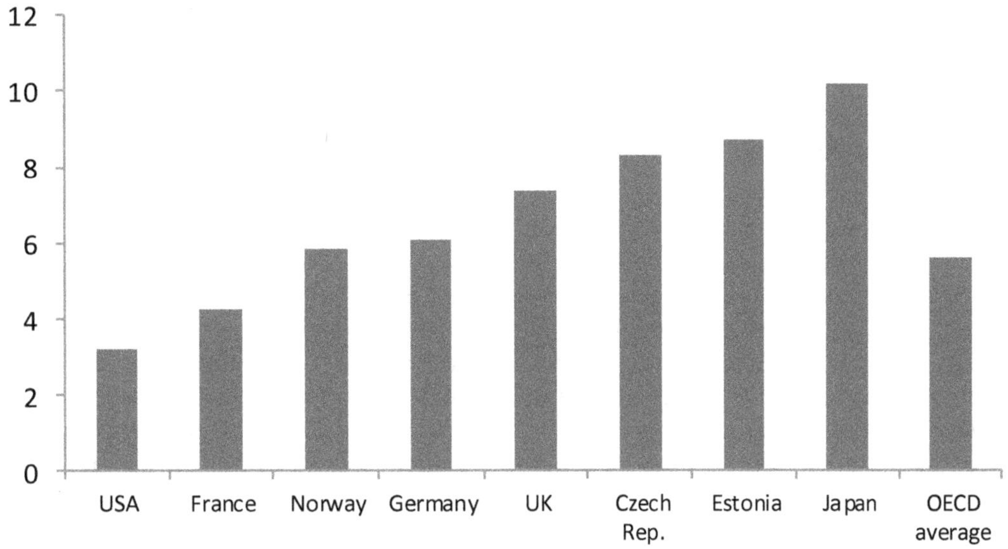

12
10
8
6
4
2
0
USA
France
Norway
Germany
UK
Czech Rep.
Estonia
Japan
OECD average

Source: OECD/EEA database on instruments used for environmental policy and natural resources management, http://www2.oecd.org/ecoinst/queries/

Figure 2.2. Revenue from environmentally-related taxes as a percentage of GDP in OECD countries, 1994-2012

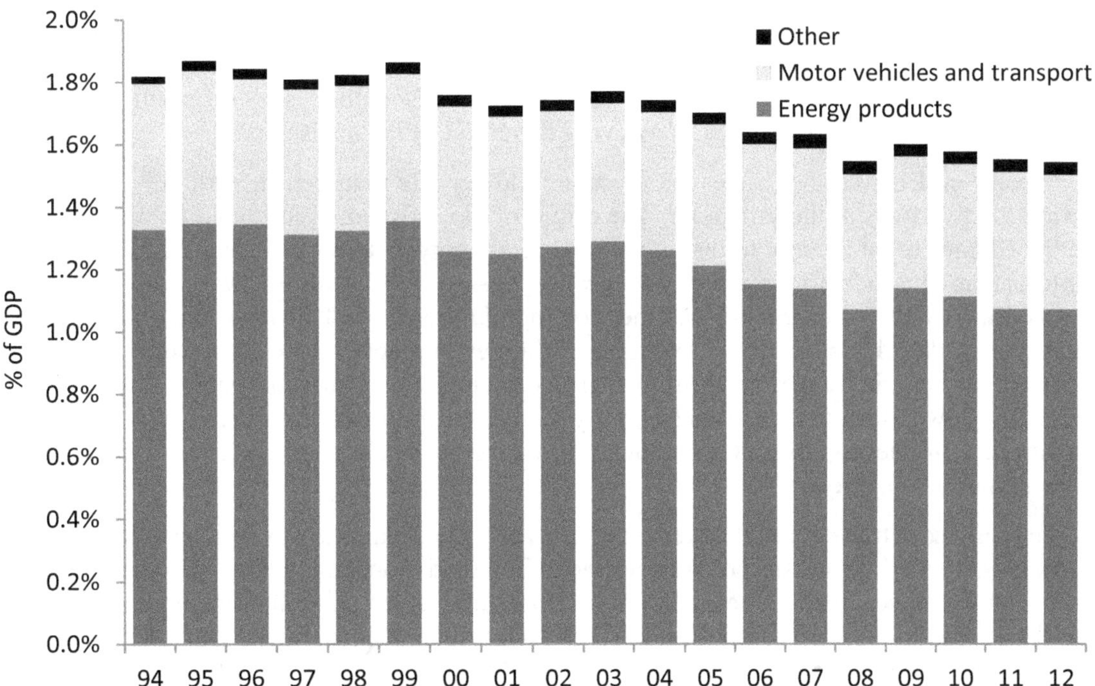

Source: OECD/EEA database on instruments used for environmental policy and natural resources management, http://www2.oecd.org/ecoinst/queries/

All EaP countries impose taxes on environmentally harmful products (such as motor fuels and imported vehicles), but only several of them have product taxes mandated by environmental legislation. A few countries differentiate the tax rates for motor fuels based on their quality. Armenia and Moldova have the most advanced systems of taxes (sometimes also referred to as charges) on environmentally harmful products. For example, Armenia imposes taxes on 29 categories of imported products and 26 categories of domestically produced ones (Armenia does not produce cars, so it only taxes imported ones), but the revenue of all its environmentally-related taxes in 2011 amounted only 0.3% of GDP.

In interpreting the revenue data shown in Figures 2.1. and 2.2. one should bear in mind that the revenue contribution of environmentally-related taxes may be a poor indication of their environmental effectiveness. Some of the most significant tax measures have achieved their environmental effects through the differentiation of an existing product tax, so that the structure of tax rates is more closely related to the environmental characteristics of the product. In this way, existing taxes have been restructured so as to introduce or sharpen environmental incentives, as for example by differentiating motor vehicle taxes according to vehicle emissions, rather than applying a uniform rate to all cars. This effect has been achieved either by increasing the tax rate on more polluting specifications of the product, or by cutting the tax rate on less polluting specifications (as with the tax reduction favouring unleaded petrol in many EU countries in the 1990s). In the latter case, the tax change may have environmental benefits, while contributing less revenue than before.

2.1.2 Taxes on motor fuels

Motor fuels are typically subject to higher taxes than other goods and services. In EU countries motor fuels – petrol and diesel – are subject to special excise taxes as well as the standard value-added tax (VAT). Motor fuel excises are levied on the basis of fuel volume (i.e. per litre) at an average rate of EUR 0.54 per litre of petrol and EUR 0.42 per litre of diesel. These excise taxes are levied before VAT is applied, so VAT applies to the price of fuel including the excise, magnifying the effect of the excise tax.

Nearly all EU Member States tax diesel at a lower rate than petrol, with only the UK taxing the two fuels at the same rate. The origin of the differential in favour of diesel can be traced back to an attempt to distinguish indirectly between motor fuels used by private motorists and by industry, and diesel was taxed less heavily because it was assumed that it was primarily used for trucks and other commercial transport. However, the differential in favour of diesel has over time encouraged the development of diesel powered private cars, which benefit from a substantial fuel tax saving. Some member states attempt to offset the lower fuel tax on diesel cars by higher taxation on the purchase or annual registration of diesel-powered cars, but this can only slightly mitigate the effects of differential fuel taxation.

In many countries, the high taxes on motor fuels are seen as a way to discourage CO_2 emissions as well as traffic congestion and other road transport-related environmental problems. However, the level of taxation of motor fuel is not set in any member state on the basis of an explicit assessment of the environmental damage caused by fuel consumption or road transport more generally. In some high-tax member states there appears to be evidence that motor fuel excises are set at a level somewhat higher than the total environmental damage and congestion cost caused by vehicle use. However, a fuel tax does not distinguish between vehicle use in different contexts, and it seems likely that vehicle use on uncongested roads is significantly overtaxed in European member states, while vehicle use on congested road-space, especially in city centres, should be taxed more heavily than at present. These effects cannot be achieved through fuel taxes, and some countries have considered the possible use of congestion charges as a better-targeted alternative instrument than heavy motor fuel taxation.

A significant fiscal development in a number of EU Member States is sharper differentiation between the taxation of fuels according to their environmental properties. In the 1980s, most European countries used a tax differential favouring unleaded petrol in order to phase out the use of leaded petrol and to accelerate the introduction of pollution-reducing catalytic converters on private cars. More recently, a number of member states have introduced lower taxes on less-damaging fuels, including low-sulphur motor fuel and biodiesel.

All EaP countries have excise taxes on motor fuels. The excise taxes on petrol are higher than those on diesel fuel in every country, as they are in the vast majority of OECD countries, but the absolute tax rates are much lower than the OECD average (Figure 2.3.) [1]. A few countries further differentiate the tax rates based on the quality (linked to the environmental characteristics) of motor fuels: for example, motor fuels that conform to Euro-4 and Euro-5 quality standards are taxed at lower rates than those fuels that do not.

Figure 2.3. Excise taxes on motor fuels in selected OECD and EaP countries, EUR per tonne

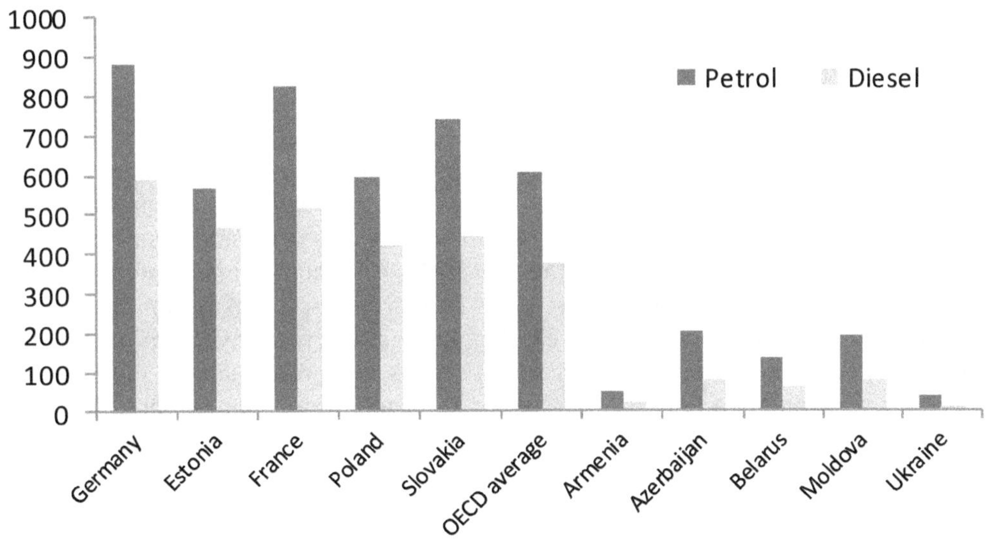

Source: EC (2013)

In addition, several countries in the region have special fuel taxes labelled as "charges on air emissions from mobile sources". These are essentially taxes that are levied on companies that produce or import motor fuels. For example, in Azerbaijan, the rate for diesel is seven times lower than for petrol. In Ukraine, these charges (differentiated for diesel based on sulphur content) were incorporated into the excise tax as of 1 January 2015.

2.1.3 Taxes on other energy products

Most OECD countries levy VAT on the sale of some other energy products besides motor fuels, including energy supplied to households and industry, although often at the reduced rate.

Given the way in which VAT operates, the VAT charged on energy supplies to industry does not provide any incentive for firms to reduce their energy use or energy-related emissions. The reason for this is that a firm which pays VAT on its production inputs, including VAT on energy supplies, can offset this VAT against the VAT bill that it has to pay on its sales. An increase in the VAT paid on the firm's purchases of energy use is thus offset by a reduction in the VAT charged on their own sales, leaving the firm indifferent to how much VAT it pays on its inputs.

In addition, many OECD countries levy excise taxes on some energy products sold to industry or households, especially heating oil. However, these are generally much lower than motor fuel excises, and are very rarely linked to the environmental aspects of energy consumption, except in the small number of countries (in Scandinavia as well as the Netherlands and Ireland) which have introduced carbon taxes.

2.1.4 Taxes on motor vehicles

Taxes levied on the sale of motor vehicles and annual taxes levied on motor vehicle ownership and use can both make a significant contribution to reducing the various adverse environmental effects associated with road transport, including local and global pollution, and also traffic congestion. The environmental impact of taxes on the sale and ownership of motor vehicles can arise in two main ways.

First, any level of taxation on cars and other motor vehicles will act to discourage vehicle ownership. Given that people with cars tend to use them for journeys that could easily be made by public transport, reducing car ownership is one of the ways in which a shift towards less-environmentally damaging public transport could be encouraged by the tax system. About three quarters of EU Member States levy an additional tax on the initial sale of motor vehicles (as well as the standard VAT), and a similar proportion levy an annual tax on vehicle ownership or use. However, these taxes on the sale and ownership of cars and other motor vehicles have until recently been rather blunt instruments for reducing adverse environmental effects. In some countries the taxes have simply been a percentage of the selling price, or an annual lump sum amount. While they may have led to some reduction in the number of vehicles purchased or used, they would have had relatively little impact on the characteristics of the vehicle stock, and in particular those characteristics affecting the environment.

Second, many of the taxes levied on the sale of motor vehicles, and annual taxes levied on motor vehicle ownership, are now structured so as to favour smaller or less-polluting vehicles. In particular, over the past decade there has been a significant increase in the number of EU countries which base these taxes, at least in part, on the CO_2 emissions from individual vehicles. Some examples are given in Box 2.1., illustrating possible models for the structure of these taxes. These incentives within the structure of motor vehicle taxes can have a much stronger environmental impact than lump-sum taxes on vehicles, or taxes based on the selling price. To the extent that they encourage vehicle purchasers to choose a car with low emissions, this impact will be felt throughout the life of the vehicle.

The environmental differentiation of car taxes in the EU has almost entirely been introduced over the last decade. It is primarily based on official measures of the emissions performance of different models of cars, and these taxes can be straightforwardly levied and enforced based on the registration of the make, model and age of the vehicle. Where some countries base their taxes on the fuel consumption of cars, this again is based on official measures for each model.

Box 2.1. Emission-based taxes on the sale or annual use of motor vehicles in selected EU countries

Austria. Supplementary taxes levied on the sale of private cars are differentiated to reflect various emissions characteristics. The starting point is a fuel consumption tax levied when a new car is first registered, which is based on the purchase price and fuel consumption. This is then supplemented by a "bonus-malus" system, in which vehicles with low CO_2 emissions receive a bonus which reduces the tax payable, while high CO2 emission vehicles pay an additional surcharge on the fuel consumption tax. A bonus is also paid to vehicles using alternative fuels. Further penalties apply to emissions of particulate matter and nitrogen oxides from diesel cars, both of which are associated with ill health in urban areas, and there are bonuses for petrol cars with low emissions of nitrogen oxides.

Finland. Both the registration tax charged on a new car and the circulation tax charged on cars each year are based on emissions of CO2. The rates at which the registration tax is charged vary between 5% and 50%, depending on emissions.

Germany. The annual circulation tax for private cars has recently been modified and now comprises a component based on cylinder capacity (EUR 2 per 100 cc for petrol engines, and EUR 9.50 per 100 cc for diesel engines) and a CO2 emissions-related component, calculated at EUR 2 per g/km in excess of 110 g/km (to fall to 95 g/km for cars registered from the start of 2014).

United Kingdom. The annual Vehicle Excise Duty has been based on CO2 emissions since 2001. The rates range from zero for cars with emissions below 100g/km to GBP 475 (EUR 555) for cars with emissions above 255 g/km. There is no supplementary tax on new cars, but since 2010 the vehicle excise duty has been charged at a higher rate in the first year of registration.

Source: Information from ACEA (2013)

In addition to the role of emissions in "standard" motor vehicle taxes, a number of countries have introduced special incentives for electric vehicles, or other innovative low-emission vehicles. Some of these incentives are delivered in the form of an exemption or substantial reduction in sale or annual use taxes, while others may achieve the same effect through direct payment of a subsidy to vehicle sellers. For example, electric vehicles are exempt from the registration tax charged on new vehicles in Belgium (Flanders), Denmark, Greece, Ireland (up to a maximum of EUR 5 000), and Latvia. Both electric and hybrid vehicles are exempt from the registration tax in Greece and Romania. Electric vehicles are exempt from both the registration tax charged on new vehicles and the annual tax in Austria, the Netherlands and Portugal.

Most EaP countries have taxes on motor vehicles, in the form of either an excise tax, a registration tax, a "transport tax" or a "road tax". However, their design is different. In Ukraine, the excise tax is differentiated based on the vehicle type, age, engine type and cylinder volume. In Moldova and Azerbaijan, the road tax is also levied on the engine volume on a progressive scale, but is annual (a similar tax in Russia is regional, and the rates increase steeply with increasing horsepower). In Armenia, there is an annual registration fee diversified by vehicle weight and the type of the vehicle's catalytic converter. Georgia uses an excise tax and an import tax, both based on the volume of the engine and the age of the vehicle and paid at the time of the vehicle's registration. In none of those countries does taxation depend on emission levels.

It should be noted that taxes on motor vehicles are limited in their potential to reduce the environmental damage caused by vehicle use. They can reduce the extent of car ownership and alter the characteristics of the vehicle stock, but they are likely to have limited effects on the cost of using a vehicle for any particular journey. Indeed, if one of the effects of environmental vehicle taxes is to encourage people to buy cars with better fuel efficiency, they may have the effect of reducing the cost of each journey, and could actually encourage more journeys rather than less.

For this reason, some policy analysts advocate measures to "diversify" car costs as much as possible: to reduce the lump-sum, one-off expenditures that car owners incur and replace them with equivalent charges per journey. It is sometimes suggested that motor vehicle insurance policies could be adjusted by making the premium depend on the number of kilometres driven, so that every journey increases the insurance premium. However, the most straightforward way of increasing the variable component in vehicle costs would be to shift away from vehicle taxes towards higher motor fuel taxes.

2.1.5 Other environmentally related product levies and taxes

A number of countries levy other environmentally-related product taxes: on batteries, tyres, pesticides and other commodities (Table 2.1.).

Table 2.1. Consumer products subject to environmentally related taxes in OECD countries

Product	Countries applying environmental tax
Household batteries	Croatia, Denmark, Hungary, Iceland, Italy, Poland, Portugal, Slovakia, Sweden
Disposable tableware	Belgium, Denmark, Latvia
Disposable cameras	Belgium
Aluminium foil	Belgium
Plastic carrier bags	Belgium, Denmark, Hungary, Ireland
Electric light bulbs	Denmark, Latvia, Slovakia
Motor vehicle batteries	Bulgaria, Iceland, Latvia, Lithuania, Poland, Portugal, Sweden
Car tyres	Bulgaria, Canada, Croatia, Denmark, Finland, Hungary, Latvia, Lithuania, Malta, Portugal, Slovakia
Paint, other solvent-containing products	Belgium, Canada
Ozone-depleting substances	Czech Republic, Poland
Pesticides	Canada, Denmark, Norway
Vehicle oils and lubricants	Canada, Croatia, Finland, Norway
Textiles	France, Denmark
Consumer electrical products	Canada, Hungary, Italy, Malta, Poland, Portugal, Slovakia

Source: OECD/EEA Economic Instruments Database, http://www2.oecd.org/ecoinst/queries/

In Denmark, a packaging tax has been levied since 1978. In its current form, the tax charged on drinks containers is volume-based, while the tax charged on other packaging products is based on weight and the environmental impact of different materials, as assessed by life-cycle analysis. Figure 2.4. shows the rates of tax levied on the principal packaging materials. The tax is paid on an equivalent basis by businesses that use packaging materials for their own products and by importers. Exports are tax-exempt to avoid damaging the international competitiveness of Danish producers. The tax, levied by the regional tax and customs administration, has proved difficult to administer because of the large number of producers involved and the complexity of its definition.

Figure 2.4.Taxes on packaging materials in Denmark, EUR per tonne

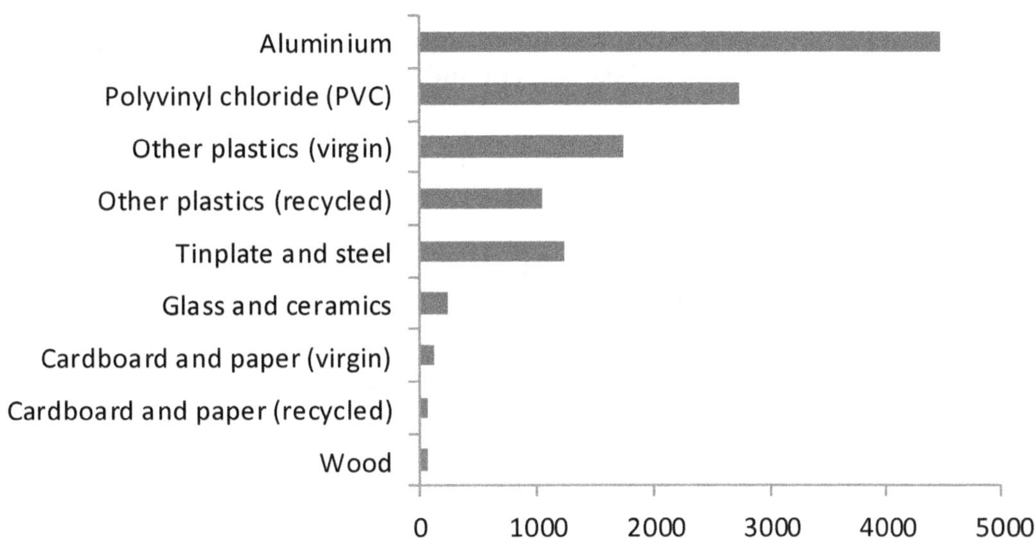

Source: Hill, J. J. Hislop and A. –E. Bégin (2008)

In Finland, a tax has been levied on drinks containers since the 1970s. In the 1990s, a differential tax applied, depending on whether the containers were to be refilled (zero tax), recycled (EUR 0.17 per litre) or discarded (EUR 0.67 per litre). In the current version of the scheme, both refillable and non-refillable containers are exempt from the tax if the producer participates in an approved deposit-refund scheme. The tax rates are high enough to have had a real incentive effect: Finland's packaging waste has been significantly below the EU average, though the removal of the tax advantage to refillables is likely to increase volumes of single-use containers.

In 2002, Ireland introduced a 15 cent tax (raised to 22 cents in 2007) on plastic shopping bags given free to customers by supermarkets and other retailers. The tax sought to reduce littering and to halt a very visible and unpopular waste of resources. Estimates of the impact on plastic bag use suggest that it had a large impact on consumer and retailer behaviour, with a dramatic 90% fall in the number of bags given free to shoppers (Convery *et al*, 2007). The response from the public and the retail industry was generally positive, with one survey in 2003 finding that the tax was supported by 91% of the population. In practical terms, the tax proved inexpensive to operate, with administrative costs absorbing only some 3% of revenues, mainly because it used the existing reporting and collection arrangements for VAT.

As mentioned earlier, Armenia and Moldova use environmentally related taxes on harmful products most extensively among EaP countries. In Armenia, the list of taxable product categories contains oil and oil products (except gasoline and diesel fuel, subject to excise taxes), batteries, asbestos-containing materials, detergents, plastic packaging, tyres and ozone-depleting substances, etc. However, it contains several inconsistencies and lacks clear definitions. In Moldova, the taxes apply only to imports of environmentally harmful products, as almost none of these products is manufactured domestically. The list of product categories was meant to be exhaustive and includes even cigarettes and chewing gum, which are not subject to environmental regulation anywhere else in the world. Toxic products (e.g. containing asbestos and lead, organic chemicals) are also part of the list, although in OECD countries they are not usually regulated through taxation (Box 2.2.).

Box 2.2. OECD recommendations on streamlining environmentally related product taxes in Moldova

The Government of Moldova should establish an Environmental Tax Reform Commission that would include the Ministry of Environment, the Ministry of Finance, the Ministry of Economy, the Customs Service, the Producers and Importers Association, etc.

The Ministry of Environment should re-evaluate the environmental rationale of each environmentally related product tax and confine the taxes to those products where the price signal can lead to behavioural change and reduced consumption and production of the taxed product. In particular, it is advisable to:

- Retain environmental taxes on the following product groups: motor fuel, fertilisers, pesticides, paints, and surface treatment agents (with appropriate tax differentiation between more and less environmentally harmful alternatives).
- Temporarily retain environmental taxes on all kinds of packaging, motor vehicles, tyres, batteries and electric bulbs. These product categories should be subject to extended producer responsibility (EPR) schemes according to the draft Law on Waste and in line with Moldova's commitment to harmonise its environmental legislation with EU Directives. However, while the EPR schemes for these products are being developed, the taxes should remain in place. Once the respective EPR schemes are fully operational, the taxes should be phased out.
- The tax on motor vehicles, currently applicable to used imported vehicles only, should be extended to new vehicles. The differentiation of excise taxes on motor vehicles based on age and/or the level of carbon dioxide emissions (and not just the engine type and size, as is currently the case) should be considered in the future.
- Eliminate environmental taxes on the following product groups: chewing gum and tobacco products and audio/video recording media (these should not be subject to environmental taxation), ozone depleting and asbestos and lead containing products (those should be banned or heavily restricted by law).

As a first step in reforming the environmental tax rates, the Government of Moldova should increase the tax rates for the retained product categories to 5% of the selling price of the least environmentally harmful alternative in the product category and to 10% of the selling price of the most environmentally harmful alternative in the product category.

Source: *OECD (2015)*

The major difference with OECD countries is in the way the tax rates are set. In Armenia and Moldova (with the exception of Moldova's tax on plastic packaging), these are *ad valorem* taxes (a percentage of the price), which is partly explained by their primary application to imported goods. In OECD countries they are usually set *ad quantum*: per kilogramme (or litre) or sometimes per item (e.g. for tyres or batteries)[2]. Therefore, it is difficult to compare most of the rates without more in-depth analysis of product prices.

2.1.6 Environmental differentiation of general product taxes

Most general sales taxes, such as VAT, operate with multiple rates. In some countries, an environmental incentive has been introduced by reclassifying polluting products to a higher-taxed category or by moving "green" products to a reduced-rate category. In the Czech Republic, a reduced rate of VAT is applied to environmentally friendly goods and services, including entrance to zoological and botanical gardens, natural reserves and national parks; public ground and water transport; municipal waste management, water supply and sewage treatment services; and fuel wood.

However, the scope for such environmental differentiation in the EU countries is limited by EU rules governing the VAT structure. One recent example has been the decision in the UK to apply reduced rates of VAT to work done by contractors to install certain energy saving materials and equipment in private housing. Environmental campaigners had pressed for this measure for a number of years, arguing that taxing energy at the reduced rate of 5% while energy-saving home improvements were taxed at the much-higher standard VAT rate created a significant tax bias against energy-saving measures. From an environmental point of view, this tax reform may have had a clear logic, but it was challenged by the European Commission because it went beyond the list of products to which a reduced-rate VAT may be applied in EU Member States.

2.2 Deposit-refund systems

The products most frequently subject to DRS are bottles, cans and other drinks containers, and a significant number of countries employ DRS for batteries. A handful of countries use DRS for motor vehicles and vehicle tyres, and some other products.

Deposit-refund systems for drinks containers, especially glass bottles, were once widespread across Europe and frequently operated on a voluntary basis by producers without any regulatory underpinning. In many countries these voluntary systems have largely disappeared, as many sellers (especially importers) have switched to single-use containers, and firms operating DRS have found them too costly to maintain in the face of intensified product market competition. In other countries, deposit-refund systems are maintained for environmental reasons, backed up by legislation to require compliance. A more recent development has been the application of DRS to single-use drinks containers, to ensure that these are collected for recycling rather than discarded as litter. Box 2.3. shows the DRS systems operated by some EU Member States, illustrating some of the models that have been employed.

In contrast, only a few deposit-refund schemes remain in place in EaP countries from the Soviet era. In Belarus and Ukraine, they are focused exclusively on glass bottles. The old system still functions in Belarus, where there are over 700 collection points for glass bottles, usually in supermarkets. In Ukraine, there is a deposit of 15 kopeks (about 1 euro cent) for 0.25 or 0.33 litre beer bottles and 20 kopeks for 0.5 litre bottles. However, a few beer producers accepting glass bottles from consumers set their own prices and do not necessarily fully refund the deposit (to increase their profit).

Box 2.3. Deposit-refund systems for drinks containers in selected EU Member States

Denmark. Legislation requires deposits to be charged on bottles and cans used for beer, soft drinks, etc. Different arrangements apply for reusable bottles and single-use packaging. Individual breweries may operate their own collection arrangements so long as they achieve a reuse rate of at least 98%. Single-use bottles and cans are collected for recycling through a deposit-refund system organised by a non-profit company, financed by charges levied on producers in proportion to their sales volume. A large number of retailers and other outlets collect items and refund deposits, including products that they themselves have not sold. The system achieved an 89% return rate for single-use packaging in 2010.

Finland. Industry-run arrangements for DRS were set up in response to the threat that a packaging tax would otherwise be introduced. There are a number of "closed" systems run by producers or retailers which collect and recycle bottles and cans from their own customers. In addition, four separate agencies run "open" deposit-refund systems for particular container types, accepting containers used by all producers.

Germany. Various producer-run systems collect reusable beer and carbonated water bottles. In addition, a universal DRS for single-use containers was established in 2003. Retailers selling drinks in disposable containers are required to take back packaging of the same material as they sell, though for smaller retailers this obligation is limited to the brands they sell themselves. The system has achieved high rates of return and recycling, of the order of 98%, but does not appear to have slowed the steady trend away from refillable bottles.

Norway. A deposit-refund system for single-use plastic bottles and cans is run by an industry-owned non-profit company. A reduced excise tax is applied if higher rates of return are achieved. About 95% of bottles and 94% of cans are collected through this system.

Source : Hill, J., J. Hislop and A.-E. Bégin (2008); EEA (2011)

Deposit-refund arrangements are used by some countries to ensure that batteries are scrapped through approved channels. Denmark introduced a DRS for nickel-cadmium (NiCd) batteries in 1996. The focus on NiCd batteries alone reflects the particularly damaging character of NiCd batteries compared with alternatives, especially their contribution to cadmium pollution, and the fact that lead batteries were already covered by an effective voluntary agreement promoting recycling. An earlier voluntary agreement on recovery of NiCd batteries had achieved inadequate rates of recovery. The NiCd battery deposit-refund system is distinctive in that it operates at the producer level, and households do not receive individual refunds. A tax is levied by the Customs and Excise Department on registered producers and importers of NiCd batteries at the rate of EUR 0.80 per battery, whether sold separately or included in a product. Refunds are made by the Danish Environmental Protection Agency to the 20 or so approved enterprises that collect used NiCd batteries at the rate of EUR 16 per kilogramme – roughly equivalent to the original tax. The system collects around 50-60% of NiCd batteries, significantly higher than the 35% collected before its introduction, when the voluntary agreement was in force. At the time of its introduction, the use of NiCd batteries had been growing at around 20% per annum, and the Danish Environmental Protection Agency believes the DRS has been effective at halting this growth.

For more than 20 years Sweden operated a deposit-refund system for motor vehicles with statutory backing. Under the 1975 Vehicle Scrapping Act a Vehicle Disposal Charge was levied when a new motor was first registered. When at the end of its life the vehicle was delivered to a vehicle dismantler for scrapping, a refund ("scrapping premium") was paid to the vehicle owner. This provided an incentive for vehicles to be scrapped through approved channels rather than dumped in the countryside or placed in the hands of unlicensed scrap merchants. For cars, the scrapping premium paid on delivery to a scrapyard was higher for older vehicles, so the refund did not always correspond to the disposal charge initially paid. The legally-mandated DRS for end-of-life vehicles was discontinued following the 1997 introduction of EPR legislation which placed a more general obligation on producers to recover vehicles and recycle materials and components, leaving them free to determine how these requirements would be achieved.

2.3 Extended Producer Responsibility

EPR schemes have spread remarkably rapidly across many countries since the early 1990s. A recent review of EPR policies commissioned by the OECD (Kaffine and O'Reilly, 2013) shows that in 1990 there were only about 20 examples across the OECD area of policy measures that involved elements of EPR. This had grown to about 100 EPR schemes by 2000, and now more than 350 schemes are in operation.

Most EPR schemes relate to groups of products, and many countries have more than one scheme in operation, each covering a different product group. More than half of the schemes cover two product groups: electronic goods (35% of schemes) and packaging (17%). Many of the remaining schemes cover motor vehicles, or various vehicle components such as tyres and batteries.

Within the EU, EPR principles have been embodied in four EU directives – relating to packaging waste, batteries, waste electrical and electronic goods and end-of-life vehicles – and subsequently transposed into the corresponding national legislation. These national EPR schemes vary widely in structure and operation. Extensive details of the operating arrangements for the various EPR schemes operated in EU Member States have recently been collected as part of an EU-funded research programme on Sustainable Management of Resources.[3]

The first EU directive to reflect EPR principles was the EU Packaging Directive (94/62/EC, amended by 2004/12/EC), which required member states to set up systems for the recovery and recycling of ***packaging waste***. The development of this directive drew heavily on the experience of Germany's path-breaking Packaging Ordinance of 1991, which required retailers and manufacturers to take back product packaging and achieve targets for recovery and recycling of different packaging materials. Many systems implemented across the EU have drawn on elements of the German model, in particular the assignment of operational responsibility to one or more PROs financed by output-related fees charged to participating firms (Box 2.4.). A small number of member states use alternative arrangements to achieve similar outcomes: the UK uses a system of tradable packaging recovery credits, while Denmark, Hungary and the Netherlands apply taxes and deposit-refund systems rather than producer-financed EPR (EC, 2012).

Separate recovery of ***batteries*** has been a priority for waste management policy, because of the potential harmful effect of the inclusion of batteries in landfilled or incinerated waste streams. The EU Directive on Batteries and Accumulators (2006/66/EC) requires member states to introduce measures to facilitate the separate collection of used batteries (consumer batteries and vehicle batteries) and places an obligation on manufacturers and importers to finance the costs of collection and recycling activities in proportion to their market share. Most member states now have operational EPR schemes for batteries.

The EU Waste Electrical and Electronic Equipment Directive (2002/96/EC) required manufacturers and importers of ***electrical and electronic goods*** to establish arrangements for the recovery and recycling of products sold after 2005 at no charge to the consumer. The directive also set weight-based collection and recycling targets for electrical goods, including a 2009 target for a minimum annual recovery rate of four kilograms of WEEE waste per head of population. Most EU countries have implemented the directive's requirements through arrangements under which recovery systems for post-2005 WEEE are producer financed, while mechanisms for financing the recovery and processing pre-2005 waste vary. The new WEEE Directive (2012/19/EC) set more ambitious collection (85%) and recycling targets and gave EU Member States the tools to fight illegal export of waste more effectively.

The EU End-of-Life Vehicles Directive (2000/53/EC) requires member states to implement EPR-based mechanisms for the recovery and recycling of ***end-of-life vehicles*** (ELVs). The majority of the schemes in member states is financed by producer contributions and levies no charge on consumers disposing of an ELV, though in some member states charges levied on vehicle sale or ownership contribute revenues to recovery and recycling operations.

There are also many examples of EPR outside the EU, including significant and varied applications in the United States, Canada and Japan, illustrating that a broad range of products can in principle be covered by EPR, including such diverse products as waste motor oil, carpets, etc.

In Canada and the United States, a wide variety of schemes for EPR – or the related concept of "product stewardship"– has been implemented, mainly at province/state level, either as a result of legislation or as an outcome of voluntary agreements at the industry level. In Canada, the products covered by EPR schemes in one or more provinces include used tyres, beverage containers, used oil (Box 2.4.), vehicle batteries, electronic waste, pharmaceuticals, paint, mercury-based thermostats and lamps, packaging and printed materials. National-level EPR schemes apply to batteries, ozone-depleting substances, obsolete pesticides and pesticide containers (Environment Canada, 2013). The schemes are generally tightly focused, with straightforward and clear mechanisms and allocation of responsibilities.

Japan's EPR scheme represents an interesting example with its principle of shared responsibility for the scheme's costs between the government, businesses and consumers. The collection of used products is undertaken by retailers, and recycling is handled by manufacturers. One distinctive feature of the scheme is the encouragement of competing industry consortia (e.g. groupings of vehicle and home appliance manufacturers) which undertake recycling and research designed to reduce long-term waste management costs. Consumers are required to pay significant fees at the time of disposal as contributions towards the costs of collection, transportation and recycling. Recovery targets are set for each category of waste, and have generally been exceeded in practice (Ogushi and Kandlikar, 2007).

International experience demonstrates a considerable diversity of practice in the organisation and financing of PROs that lie at the heart of EPR schemes. In EU countries, PROs have tended to be industry-run bodies, often set up under the auspices of an industry association, and there has been an increasing tendency in recent years for countries to encourage the development of multiple PROs handling the wastes in a particular product area, with the aim of securing greater efficiency in PRO operations through competition. In some cases, new PROs have been set up by a group of firms which have seen the opportunity for greater efficiency, and hence for a lower financial burden, if they leave the existing PRO.

Box 2.4. Examples of EPR schemes in OECD countries

EPR for packaging in Germany. The main scheme (introduced in 1991) covers only household packaging (glass, tinplate, aluminium and paper/cardboard – single-use beverage containers are covered by a separate DRS), but not industrial packaging. Since 2003, companies that bring packaging to the market can choose from several PROs. Producers pay fees to the PRO per amount of packaging material put on the market, the PRO then pays for the collection, recovery and recycling, and use of municipal space for collection containers. In 2011, the household packaging recovery rate for all materials was 80%, and the recycling rate was 75%. The scheme has high consumer acceptance due to the convenient collection infrastructure, active environmental education campaigns, and financial incentives for households (who save on waste collection fees by reducing the volume of non-recoverable waste).

EPR for packaging in the UK. The scheme, introduced in 1997, requires producers collectively to meet a target for the percentage of packaging waste to be recovered and recycled, which is translated into targets for each individual company. Companies have the option of meeting their target through their own actions or by signing up to one of several registered "compliance schemes" which undertake recovery and recycling on behalf of their member companies. Compliance is demonstrated by "Packaging Waste Recovery Notes" (PRNs) – certificates for each ton of packaging material recycled. PRNs are tradable, allowing compliance schemes and companies to meet their recycling targets either through their own collection and recycling operations or through the purchase of certificates from others who have exceeded their targets. The overall recycling rate for packaging waste was 62% in 2011.

EPR for packaging in the Czech Republic. EKO-KOM is the PRO for packaging waste, although producers can choose individual producer responsibility. EKO-KOM collects producer contributions of EUR 20 per ton of packaging put on the market, reimburses municipalities for the collection of household packaging waste, and contracts waste management companies to ensure proper treatment and recycling of the collected packaging. Producers of industrial packaging are responsible for collection and treatment. The recycling targets are differentiated by material (e.g. 70% for glass and 37% for plastic) and are increased every year. The 91% overall collection rate and 71% recycling rate were achieved in 2012.

EPR for batteries in Austria. Four PROs (one for-profit and three non-profit organisations) are responsible for arranging the take-back and treatment of waste portable batteries, and all of them are also part of the WEEE scheme. A fifth PRO covers only automotive batteries. A producer not participating in a PRO scheme may get a fine of double the amount they would have to pay to a PRO. Portable batteries are collected at municipal collection facilities or at the point of sale. A collection rate of about 50% has been reached for portable batteries.

EPR for WEEE in Sweden. The WEEE collection system is based on two schemes: (1) an agreement between Swedish municipalities and El-Kretsen, an organisation of producers of electronic products, that the municipalities will bear all costs of collecting electric waste while El-Kretsen will pay for their treatment and recycling; and (2) a collection scheme operated by the Association for Recycling Electronic Products with collection points in its members' stores. Several producers have individual schemes. Producers adhering to a PRO must pay an annual fee based on the number of products sold and their recycling costs.

EPR for waste oils in Canada. The Western Canada Used Oil Program (operating in four provinces) employs EPR to ensure recovery and safe disposal of used motor oil as a way to prevent damaging discharges into sewers, watercourses and groundwater. Sales and imports of oil are subject to a fee, or "environmental handling charge", which is then used to finance a "return incentive" paid to authorised collectors when used oil is collected and recycled (e.g. into heating oil). The scheme has close similarities with a conventional DRS, with the significant exception that refunds are paid not to consumers but the enterprises that collect used oil, providing them with an incentive to maximise the amount collected.

Source: EC (2014); Salmons, R. (2002); Walls, M. (2004)

EaP countries are increasingly interested in developing EPR schemes. An EPR scheme has recently been introduced in Belarus while some EPR elements exist in Ukraine (Box 2.5.). These schemes cover an ambitiously wide range of products and envisage the establishment of a single state-owned PRO, but the fees levied on producers and importers are insufficient to cover the collection, treatment and recycling costs. As a result, in practice these schemes so far appear to be ineffective. In Moldova, an EPR scheme is being designed at the time of the writing for five priority waste streams: WEEE, ELVs, used oil, batteries and packaging waste[4].

Box 2.5. Emerging EPR schemes in EaP countries

Belarus. The EPR scheme was introduced in 2012 and covers 17 product categories, including packaging, used oil, tyres, household appliances, electrical and electronic equipment, electric bulbs, batteries, etc. Producers and importers can organise their own collection, processing and recycling systems that would have to meet the 30% recycling target for packaging, used oil, tyres and disposable tableware, and the 10% recycling target for the other product categories covered by the EPR. Alternatively, they must sign a contract for these services with the single nationwide, state-owned, non-profit operator for those services and pay it a fee that is set either as a percentage of the sale price of electrical and electronic equipment, batteries, electric bulbs and lubricating oils, or as a fixed charge, different for different kinds of packaging materials (plastic, cardboard and glass).

Ukraine. A 2001 Government Resolution on the collection, processing and reuse of *packaging waste* created a state-owned Ukrecoresursy company and put it in charge of managing the scheme. It set fees (per kg) for the collection and processing of paper, cardboard, plastic, glass, tin and aluminium packaging, revenues from which should be collected on a special treasury account and managed by the government. In practice, only importers paid a nominal fee to Ukrecoresursy (domestic producers remain unaffected), which, however, undertook very little recycling activity. In March 2015, the Government repealed its resolution and abolished Ukrecoresursy. As of June 2015, a new draft Law on Packaging and Packaging Waste has been developed by the Ministry of Ecology and Natural Resources which would establish an industry-owned PRO to ensure compliance with packaging recovery rates stipulated by the government.

A 2012 Government Resolution targeted the collection, processing and disposal of *used industrial oils*, setting the same obligation for enterprises and a minimum fee of 7 euro cents per litre. It also approved special rules for the collection, processing and disposal of used oils, establishing such terms as “authorised enterprise” (a state-owned entity managing the scheme) and “specialised enterprise” (performing the technical operations). It set a mandatory recycling target of 40% of the volume of oil used, but the system to-date remains dysfunctional.

An EPR scheme for *tyres* introduced in 2011 is not operational either due to the lack of regulations on the collection, processing and reuse of old tyres, and associated fees for producers and importers.

Notes

1 In case of tax differentiation between quality grades of petrol in EaP countries, the highest tax rate was used.

2 There are very few examples of ad valorem product taxes, including the tax on pesticides in Denmark and the tax on plastic packaging in Poland.

3 https://sites.google.com/a/eu-smr.eu/guidance-on-epr/documents

4 The principal alternatives considered are either (a) to give producers a right to establish their organisations and systems for the collection, processing, and recycling of products; or (b) to introduce fees for producers and importers, with revenues channelled into a state-managed fund, which would in turn contract waste management companies (following the Czech example, Box 2.4.).

References

ACEA (2013), Tax Guide 13: European Union. Brussels: European Automobile Manufacturers' Association, www.acea.be/images/uploads/files/20130326_TaxGuide2013Highlights.pdf

Convery, Frank J., Simon McDonnell and Susana Ferreira (2007), *The most popular tax in Europe? Lessons from the Irish plastic bags levy*, Environmental and Resource Economics, 38 (1), pp.1-11.

Environment Canada (2013), *Inventory of Extended Producer Responsibility and Product Stewardship Programs,* www.ec.gc.ca/gdd-mw/default.asp?lang=En&n=9FB94989-1

EC (2014), *Development of Guidance on Extended Producer Responsibility Final Report,* Produced by BIO Intelligence Service (Deloitte), http://ec.europa.eu/environment/archives/waste/eu_guidance/index.html.

EC (2013), *Excise Duty Tables, Part II: Energy products and electricity,* Ref1038rev1, July 2013. http://ec.europa.eu/taxation_customs/index_en.htm#.

EEA (2011), *European Refunding Scheme for Drinks Containers. Report*, Co-rapporteurs Mr. Nikolai Astrup and Ms. Anna Hedh, Ref 1109540, 26 October 2011, Joint Parliamentary Committee, European Environment Agency.

EU (2012), *Directive 2012/19/EU of the European Parliament and of the Council of 4 July 2012 on waste electrical and electronic equipment*, European Commission.

EU (2006), *Directive 2006/66/EC of the European Parliament and of the Council of the 6 September 2006 on batteries and accumulators and repealing Directive 91/157/EEC*, European Commission.

EU (2004), *Directive 94/62/EC of the European Parliament and Council of 20 December 1994 on packaging and packaging waste, OJ L 365, 1994, p. 10, as amended by Directive 2004/12/EC of the European Parliament and Council of 11 February 2004*, European Commission.

EU (2002), *Directive 2002/96/EC of the European Parliament and of the Council of 27 January 2003 on waste electrical and electronic equipment*, European Commission.

EU (2000), *Directive 2000/53/EC of the European Parliament and of the Council of 18 September 2000 on end-of-life vehicles*, European Commission.

EU (1992a), *Council Directive 92/81/EEC of 19 October 1992 on the harmonisation of the structures of excise duties on mineral oils*, European Commission.

EU (1992b), *Council Directive 92/82/EEC of 19 October 1992 on the approximation of the rates of excise duties on mineral oils*, European Commission.

Hill, J., H. Hislop and A.-E. Bégin (2008), *Good product, bad product? Making the case for product levies*, Green Alliance, February 2008.

Kaffine, D. and P. O'Reilly (2013), *What Have We Learned About Extended Producer Responsibility in the Past Decade? A Survey of the Recent EPR Economic Literature*, mimeo, 24 May 2013.

MS2 (2011), *Best Practice International Packaging Approaches*, Report by Martin Stewardship and Management Strategies Pty Ltd, Turramurra, NSW Australia. November 2011, www.scew.gov.au.

Ogushi, Y. and M. Kandlikar (2007), *Assessing Extended Producer Responsibility Laws in Japan*, Environmental Science and Technology, July 1, 2007, pp 4502-4508.

OECD (2015), *Economic instruments for managing environmentally harmful products in Moldova: Current practices and policy recommendations*, OECD, Paris.

OECD (2004), *Environmental Pollution and Product Charges in Armenia: Assessment of Reform Progress and Directions for Further Improvement*, OECD, www.oecd.org/countries/armenia/34500203.pdf .

Salmons, R. (2002), "*New Areas for Application of Tradeable Permits - Solid Waste Management*" in OECD (2002), Implementing Domestic Tradeable Permits: Recent Developments and Future Challenges, OECD Publishing, Paris, http://dx.doi.org/10.1787/9789264191983-en.

Walls, M. (2004), "EPR policy goals and policy choices: What does economics tell us?", in *Economic Aspects of Extended Producer Responsibility*, OECD Publishing, Paris, http://dx.doi.org/10.1787/9789264105270-en.

3. Product taxes and environmental tax differentiation: Design and implementation

New environmentally related product taxes or the differentiation of existing taxes such as VAT or excise taxes can both be used to create incentives for environmental improvement. Successful introduction of well-functioning environmentally related product taxes will generally require close co-ordination between different branches of government, in particular between the environment ministry and the ministry of finance. There are several possible ways to implement environmentally related product taxes. This section addresses such implementation issues as revenue raising, competitiveness and income distribution concerns.

3.1 Incentives for behavioural change

The environmental policy case for environmental product taxation is the potential it has to promote the production and use of "greener" products and to steer economic activity in a direction that causes less environmental damage.

Environmental product taxes have two main channels of potential influence:

- First, if higher taxes on "dirty" products are passed on in higher prices for these products, compared with lower-taxed "green" products, this will tend to alter consumer choices, leading to a direct switch to greener products. The scale of this change in consumer purchasing will depend on the level of the environmental product tax and on the relative pre-tax prices of green and dirty products.
- Second, producers may also be stimulated to produce or develop cleaner products because they will be subject to less tax.

The area of the economy that has seen the greatest use of environmentally related taxes is the production and consumption of fossil fuels. As noted earlier, taxes on energy products – predominantly motor fuel taxes – constitute about two thirds of all environmentally related taxation in OECD countries, measured in terms of revenue. There are substantial opportunities for taxes on energy products to steer production and consumption in a less environmentally damaging direction, for example by encouraging substitution to less-polluting fuels, by encouraging the use of more fuel-efficient energy-using equipment and vehicles, by encouraging a shift towards greater use of public transport, by discouraging consumption of energy-intensive products and services, and so on.

Examples of other products where there is scope for environmentally related product taxes to encourage consumer and producer switching to environmentally better alternatives include:

- ***Disposable products*** such as cameras, tableware, etc.;
- ***Pesticides and fertilizers.*** Higher taxes on pesticides and fertilizers can act to discourage their excessive application by making these products sufficiently expensive that they are used selectively rather than indiscriminately;
- ***Batteries***. Higher taxes on the most environmentally damaging types of batteries could encourage switching to less-damaging alternatives. Higher taxes on all forms of disposable batteries could encourage greater use of rechargeable batteries;
- ***Packaging materials***. High taxes on all packaging materials might encourage a reduction in excessive product packaging. Selective taxation of the most damaging forms of packaging (e.g. composite materials which cannot be recycled) would encourage a switch to less-damaging (recyclable) packaging;
- ***Electrical products*** with large end-of-life costs; and
- ***Incandescent light bulbs***. High taxes on traditional incandescent light bulbs, which are cheap but very energy-inefficient, could tip the balance of consumer choices towards more expensive but energy-efficient alternatives.

The great advantage of promoting behavioural change through environmentally related product taxes is that it may achieve environmental improvements at lower cost to the economy than other available instruments. Using price incentives by taxing "dirty" goods more than "green" alternatives allows for more flexibility in producer and consumer responses. Taxes encourage behavioural change but do not force change when it would be excessively costly. In this way, they ensure that environmental policy can be effective without excessive cost.

In theory, emissions taxes provide an attractive alternative to product-based taxes. If based on measured emissions of a pollutant, they can be targeted precisely to environmental damage and can provide clear incentives for reduced damage: a firm which reduces its emissions will reduce the amount of tax it pays. However, the practical use of emissions taxes in OECD countries has been confined to a relatively limited number of areas – principally air pollutants from power stations and water effluents. One reason for the rather restricted application of emissions taxes is that they require measurement of actual emissions, which typically entails significant costs of installation and operation of emission measurement equipment, and the associated reporting and verification.

In fact, in certain cases product-based taxes can achieve outcomes which are as good as those from direct taxation of emissions. These are cases where a product can be taxed on a basis which precisely reflects the emissions associated with its production or consumption. One important example of this is the use of taxes on energy products to reflect the carbon dioxide emissions that would result when they are used. Where taxes are levied on some component of the content of a product (e.g. the sulphur content of fuels), they may provide a reasonable approximation to subsequent polluting emissions.

3.1.1 Tax rate

In theory, the rate at which an environmentally related product tax should be set should reflect the environmental damage caused by the product or activity in question. In practice, most countries that have introduced environmentally related taxes on products have not based the tax rate on an explicit assessment of the damage caused by each unit sold. This largely reflects the difficulty of making such assessments.

What tax rate is needed to achieve a switch to less environmentally damaging production and consumption behaviour? This depends on the products in question. Where there are close "green" substitutes for the dirty product, a given rate of tax may encourage a large proportion of consumers to switch to the green alternative and, likewise, producers would be more likely to switch away from producing the taxed dirty product. Where the alternatives are less satisfactory or more costly to produce, less switching is likely.

The tax rate needs to be large enough to make a real difference in the price of the dirty product, so that consumers notice the difference, and producers see a strong reason to change what they produce. It is unlikely that a tax rate of less than about 10% will achieve any significant behavioural change in consumer purchasing or firms' production decisions, and environmental product taxes are unlikely to be worth introducing unless they are levied at 10% or more. On the other hand, taxes on products that are higher than about 20% of the product price may be difficult to administer and enforce because they risk provoking substantial tax evasion, except where the product is subject to close monitoring and control, as in the case of mineral oils and motor vehicles. This suggests that, as a matter of general guidance, the additional environmental product tax rate on "dirty" products should in most cases lie within a range of 10 to 20% of the product price.

While it is unlikely to be possible to assess exactly how this compares with the environmental damage caused by each unit consumed, the aim should be to confine such taxes to products that are associated with significant environmental damage, so that the scale of the tax is not disproportionate to the environmental damage associated with production or consumption of the product.

Once the initial tax rates are set taking account of the environmental considerations and revenue implications, it may be appropriate to maintain these tax rates for some time – there are a number of examples in OECD countries' practice where initial rates of environmentally related taxation have not changed for a number of years. However, inflation and other environmental and economic changes will require a procedure for revising the rates.

3.1.2 Targeting

If the aim of the incentive is to change behaviour, it is important that the incentive be accurately "targeted" to the underlying environmental problem, because poorly targeted taxes can impose costs without achieving the desired behavioural changes. The tax needs to be charged at a higher level on "dirty" products than on the "green" alternatives if it is to change the decisions of consumers and producers in favour of the green alternatives. In some cases this may be easy to achieve through differentiation of existing sales taxes (e.g. differentiation of an excise tax on fuel based on its sulphur content), while in other cases accurate targeting may be harder to achieve.

Much depends on how accurately the tax system can distinguish between "green" and "dirty" products, so that higher taxes apply to the latter only. In some cases, identifying the products that should be taxed more heavily is straightforward. Taxes on fossil fuels used by households provide a clear incentive to use less fuel and to invest in energy efficiency measures (better insulation, etc.) that will reduce fossil fuel consumption. In this way, such taxes can provide well-targeted incentives to reduce carbon dioxide emissions from household energy consumption.

In other cases, it may not be easy, as a practical matter, to distinguish between the products that should be subject to an environmental product tax and those to which it should not apply. In practice, for example, it may be difficult to tax sales of paper made from virgin pulp more heavily than recycled paper, since it would be necessary for the taxing authorities to investigate the life history of the products in order to be able to apply the correct rate of tax. At the point where the tax is applied, paper from virgin pulp may look close to indistinguishable from recycled paper.

In another group of cases, the tax structures that are feasible may not accurately reflect the complex pattern of environmental costs caused by individual consumption. High taxes on motor vehicles and motor fuels are frequently used to reflect the environmental costs generated by private vehicle use. However, some of these costs depend on aspects of individual consumption that cannot be reflected in a tax. Thus, for example, some motor vehicle exhaust emissions (e.g. of particulates from diesel engines) are highly damaging in urban areas, where they can harm the health of many people in a densely-settled area, but cause much less human health damage in rural areas, simply because there are fewer people to be harmed. On the other hand, diesel cars typically generate lower emissions of carbon dioxide per kilometre driven than petrol-engine cars and, therefore, cause less climate change damage. Ideally, environmental policy should aim to reduce diesel car use in urban areas, but this is not something that can be accurately incentivised by taxes on vehicles and fuels.

A further aspect of efficient targeting of the tax incentive is the form that an environmentally-based product tax should take, and in particular the choice between *ad valorem* taxes, levied as a percentage of the product price, and "specific" or *ad quantum* taxes, levied on the basis of the quantity of the product. Most existing general sales taxes (such as VAT) are levied on an ad valorem basis, i.e. on the value of goods sold. By contrast, many of the excise taxes which countries levy on mineral oils and other products are based on the quantity of the product. One strong practical reason for this is that such excise taxes are typically levied at a stage in the production and distribution chain when the final selling price cannot be easily observed.

Generally, the environmental harm caused by dirty products is a function of the quantity produced or consumed rather than its price. Lower quality, cheaper, versions of a product may cause just as much environmental harm, and possibly more, during production or consumption as more expensive versions. If the tax is to be levied on a basis which reflects the scale of environmental harm, taxes based on quantity (e.g. litres of motor fuel) will be a better targeted incentive than an increased *ad valorem* tax on dirty products. This suggests that the scope for using existing taxes to introduce environmental incentives will be greatest in areas where excise taxes are currently levied. The excise taxes on motor fuels could, for example, be differentiated to reflect sulphur content, and excise taxes on motor vehicles could be charged according to the emissions performance of different models. EaP countries that have ad valorem taxes on environmentally harmful products should consider shifting the tax base to the quantity of these products.

3.1.3 Tax differentiation

The most straightforward way of using environmental product taxes to discourage consumption of environmentally-damaging products is simply to levy a tax on these products. Many of the applications of environmental product taxation in OECD countries have taken this form. However, it is possible that a more complex policy could provide stronger incentives for changes in production and consumption that would result in a greater environmental improvement.

One more complex policy approach would be environmentally motivated tax differentiation, which would simultaneously increase the tax on "dirty" goods while at the same time reducing the existing rates of taxation (e.g. VAT or other sales taxes) on the "green" alternative. Higher taxes could be imposed on single-use batteries, for example, while the existing VAT on rechargeable batteries could be cut. The effect would be to increase the tax advantage in favour of rechargeable batteries, and hence the incentive to switch to the greener product would be strengthened.

Tax differentiation of this form effectively uses some or all of the revenue raised from the higher environmental product tax to finance a tax cut for the green alternative. Another way to achieve the same incentive for consumers to switch to the green alternative would be a still higher tax on the "dirty" good, and this could be done without foregoing tax revenues from sales of the "green" good. However, there are practical limits to how high a rate of tax can be set without stimulating excessive evasion and false accounting, as well as political limits to how high the rate of tax can be set on any product without excessive producer and voter resistance. The combination of tax increases on "dirty" goods and tax reductions on some "green" goods may then be a more politically palatable approach.

3.1.4 Evaluation of effectiveness

A significant part of the rationale for product-based environmentally related taxes is that they can change behaviour, especially the behaviour of consumers, in ways that are less costly than more inflexible forms of product regulation, or direct environmental regulation of polluting activities. In general, however, these effects are likely to be difficult to observe, for a number of reasons. First, adjustments in consumer behaviour are likely to be gradual. Consumers may make decisions on the basis of habit and may take time to notice price differentials created by differential taxation. Consumption of motor fuels, for example, is very heavily determined by vehicle ownership decisions, including the type and size of car owned, and the full response to changes in fuel taxes will not occur until the consumer buys a new car. Second, many environmentally related tax measures are introduced as part of a policy package with other related measures, and it is difficult to disentangle the separate effect of the tax change alone. Third, there may be other changes in economic conditions or technologies which will change consumer purchasing at the same time. For these reasons, there are relatively few assessments of the actual impact of environmentally related tax measures.

Rather more evidence exists on the likely impact of such measures, based on wider evidence of how consumption responds to changes in prices. Thus, for example, straightforward increases in the rates of motor fuel taxes will be likely to have effects on the consumption of motor fuel that can be inferred from the evidence on the "elasticity" (price responsiveness) of motor fuel consumption to more general changes in fuel prices. As would be expected, given the important role of vehicle ownership in determining fuel consumption, this is relatively modest in the short term, but becomes significantly larger once the full set of consumer adjustments take place, including changes in vehicle ownership patterns.

3.2 Design issues

There are ranges of possible ways to implement environmentally related product taxes. One option makes use of existing product taxes (sales taxes) and achieves an environmental effect through a change in tax rates within the existing system. Another option implements environmentally related product taxes separately from existing sales tax arrangements. The first question of practical design that needs to be addressed is the extent to which the introduction of an environmentally related product tax can draw on existing taxation arrangements and be incorporated within the administration of existing taxes, especially sales taxes.

This decision needs to balance the requirements of environmental effectiveness and efficient fiscal administration:

- To be environmentally effective, the product tax needs to apply to clearly identified products that are associated with environmental damage in the course of production or consumption while not taxing products that are not associated with environmental damage, and to be levied at a high enough rate.
- Efficient fiscal administration requires that the tax be levied without requiring excessively high administrative costs to government or excessive costs of bureaucracy to taxpayers. A key consideration is that the environmentally related product tax should not jeopardise the efficient administration of other parts of the tax system.

Full administrative integration

Introducing environmental incentives into the structure of an existing product tax system has the potential to create environmentally related product taxes without incurring the costs of setting up and running an additional, separate tax administration. Differentiating the rates of an existing sales tax so that a higher rate of tax is applied to a list of "dirty" goods provides a simple and potentially low-cost route to implementing environmentally related product taxes.

Tax differentiation within an existing system of product taxes has the drawback that the environmental product tax cannot be specified with a completely free hand. It would be necessary to respect constraints arising from the structure and operation of the existing tax system. For example, where environmentally related product taxes are to be incorporated within a sales tax such as VAT, they have to take the form of a percentage of the selling price of the product because that is how VAT works. This limitation may, however, be acceptable, as it avoids the need to incur the costs of setting up and operating a wholly new independent system to run the tax.

Each of the existing product taxes could be adapted as the basis for introducing environmentally related product taxes, either by differentiating the rates of tax currently applied or by more complex reforms.

VAT covers the widest range of commodities and transactions but is the least flexible of the existing product tax systems in terms of its ability to accommodate the requirements of additional environmentally related product taxes.

- VAT is a price-based tax, so any environmentally related product tax incorporated within the VAT would need to take this form. Environmental damage may not always be well related to the price of a product. Cheap brands of some product might cause as much environmental damage as more expensive brands, but with VAT the tax will always have to be a fixed percentage of the price.
- Multiple tax rates within a VAT system sharply increase the cost of administration as both taxpayers and the tax authorities can no longer focus simply on the aggregate value of sales by a business. They would need to collect and verify information on sales subject to each of the different tax rates and a firm's purchases in each of the different tax rate categories. The amount of reported information rises sharply, and new opportunities open up for highly-profitable tax evasion by misreporting sales into a lower-taxed category, a form of evasion that is very difficult to control from purely accounts-based tax audit methods.
- VAT is really only effective at introducing incentives for changes in consumer behaviour and cannot discourage the use of environmentally damaging products ***in the course of production***. The reason is that VAT is essentially designed to tax sales to final consumers only. It does this implicitly, by giving credit (i.e. refund) for taxes paid on a firm's purchases of taxed goods and services. The effect of this is to leave businesses indifferent to the rate of VAT they pay on purchased inputs, since they effectively reclaim that tax when they are taxed on their sales. Whether this limitation matters depends on the nature of the environmental problem being addressed, and whether other, supplementary, approaches are available to deal with this issue.

In most countries ***excise taxes*** are levied on a limited number of commodities, but these include some of considerable environmental significance, especially motor fuels and vehicles.

- Taxes on motor fuels are often already high compared to other goods and services, but their environmental impact could be enhanced by levying additional taxation on "dirty" varieties of the product (e.g. high-sulphur motor fuel) or reducing tax on its "green" varieties (e.g. unleaded petrol).
- In practical terms, motor fuel excises are generally single-stage taxes levied at a defined point in the production and distribution process. Usually this is well before the retail stage to ensure effective enforcement and low costs of administration. Often excises are levied at the point where motor fuels leave the refinery or large-scale distribution facilities. Up to this point, production and distribution are closely monitored by the revenue authorities to ensure that untaxed output does not escape into the retail system. Once the excise has been levied, the expectation is that it will be largely passed forward in higher prices at each subsequent sale until it reaches the final consumer.
- Because they are levied well before the point of retail sale, at a stage where no market transaction may be taking place, fuel excises are generally based on product quantity (litres) rather than price. This has some advantages when it comes to environmental differentiation, since it is generally quantity rather than value that is most closely related to environmental damage.

Import duties provide a third option for integrating environmentally related product taxes with existing taxation.

- In many countries, oil and refined oil products are mainly imported, and taxation at the border can be a substitute for excises levied on domestic production. Indeed, if there is no domestic production, the system may be based entirely on taxation at the point of import. If border formalities are effectively enforced, this may be the cheapest way to levy a high rate of tax without provoking large-scale evasion.
- WTO rules generally require that any environmentally related product taxes apply equally to both domestic production and equivalent imports. Such taxes should not be used as an indirect way of introducing trade protection to favour domestic production over imports. This limits the extent to which the administrative arrangements for import duties can be useful in setting up a system of environmentally related product taxation, since provide no mechanism for levying an equivalent tax on domestic producers.

Stand-alone operation

Where it is impossible to integrate an environmentally related product tax into the structure and administration of existing sales taxation, it may be necessary to consider a stand-alone system of environmental product taxes, levied on one or more products that damage the environment in the course of their production or use. This is potentially costly, requiring administrative operations that may duplicate many which are already undertaken for the existing product taxes. However, it does have the advantage that the tax could be designed in the way most appropriate to the environmental problem being addressed, largely unconstrained by other tax policy choices or by existing administrative structures and processes.

In practice, a significant proportion of the environmentally related product taxes operated in OECD countries are largely independent of the main product taxes. One reason is that they can then be levied on the basis of attributes more directly related than product price to environmental performance, as in the taxes levied in Denmark on the basis of weight.

Stand-alone operation of an environmental product tax would require the following:

- ***Identification of relevant producers and importers***. Legislation could require producers and importers of certain commodities to register, and these declarations could then be used as the basis for identifying potential taxpayers. Some resources would need to be devoted to tracking down firms that have failed to register. It would be desirable to make firms liable indefinitely for any tax arrears due to a failure to register, plus a significant additional penalty.
- ***Periodic (annual or quarterly) taxpayer returns*** of amounts sold of each of the commodities subject to the environmental product tax.
- ***Significant audit and investigation resources*** need to be deployed to verify the accuracy of these taxpayer returns. The competent authority needs to be given appropriate powers to obtain access to the firms' financial and sales records on a basis equivalent to the powers held by the principal tax agency.
- ***Assessment of the tax due***. There is a significant move in international tax administration towards giving taxpayers the initial responsibility for calculating the tax due and depositing a corresponding payment with the tax authorities. This speeds up the process.
- ***Arrangements for tax payment***. Taxpayers need to have an incentive for early payment, which can be given by charging an appropriate interest rate on late payments. If subsequent investigation demonstrates that additional tax has been due, the tax agency needs to have powers to collect it and to levy an appropriate penalty for the initial under-payment.

Even where the operation of the tax is wholly separate from the operation of existing taxes, there are good reasons to design the operations of the environmental product tax to mirror those employed in the existing tax administration. This means that experienced staff can be hired from the existing tax authority, increasing the chances that the new system can be established quickly and effectively. Following the administrative practice of existing taxes reduces the risk that taxpayers will be confused by different procedures for different taxes.

Intermediate options

Between the two extremes of full integration and wholly separate administration, there are a range of intermediate possibilities in which a new product tax could be introduced, making use of aspects of the operation of other existing taxes while not being fully integrated within the existing tax system. These could include:

- Subcontracting the administration of the environmental product tax to the agency collecting the general product tax, without any legislative integration. The tax authority would then administer and collect two taxes. Combining certain activities (e.g. tax inspection) would achieve some efficiencies compared with two parallel tax systems administered entirely separately. Arrangements would need to be made to share the operating costs between the two systems.

- Information exchange or pooling between the general tax authority and the environmental product tax administration. It would be very useful to an agency trying to run a stand-alone system of environmental product taxes to receive from the general tax authority a list of firms involved in the relevant industry. It might also be useful for both authorities to share information about the level and pattern of activities of the firms that they both tax, since information gathered by one authority may be useful to the other administration. Both, for example, would obtain information about the level and pattern of firms' production and sales, and sharing this information allows for some cross-checking.
- Separate assessment of the environmental product tax and the general sales tax, but combined tax collection, payments processing and enforcement.

3.3 Revenue considerations

Environmentally related product taxes raise revenues. In some cases, especially with taxes levied at high rates on motor vehicles and fuels, these revenues can be substantial. In other cases, where the rates are lower and the sales of the taxed commodity are smaller, the revenues may be quite modest.

The revenue obtained from an environmental product tax is affected by any behavioural responses to the tax. If the tax succeeds in encouraging consumers to shift away from the taxed "dirty" goods to less environmentally damaging products, this will reduce the revenue. These changes in consumer behaviour may take some time to occur, so the revenues from environmentally related product taxes may diminish over time.

Revenues from environmentally related product taxes are also affected by changes over time in the tax rates and in economic conditions. The most important of these is the effect of inflation. One strong advantage of taxes that are levied as a percentage of the selling price of a product is that they increase automatically when the price of the product rises. Taxes levied on the basis of product quantity, such as motor fuel taxes levied per litre, need to be deliberately adjusted each year in other to keep pace with inflation. This process of regular adjustment can introduce considerable unpredictability into the level of the tax and its revenues, especially if the adjustment of tax rates becomes a matter of political discussion and controversy. There is a real danger that the tax may be steadily eroded through inflation, if legislators are unwilling to be seen to be voting regularly for tax increases. With taxes that are levied as a percentage of price, the inflation adjustment is automatic, and tax increases may be less controversial.

The use of revenues generated by environmental product taxes varies. The revenues from high rates of tax on motor fuels and other energy products are of real significance to the overall public revenue in many countries and are not allocated to any particular environmental purpose.

Revenues from smaller environmental product taxes are sometimes "earmarked" to an environmental budget line. In some cases this may be a fund related to the disposal of the product concerned. Some countries, for example, levy taxes on the sale of certain products to cover the eventual costs that will be incurred in end-of-life waste management and disposal costs. This includes cases where product charges are levied in order to fund industry-run agencies handling collection and disposal of end-of-life products under EPR, as discussed in Chapter 5.

Revenue earmarking has advantages as well as some drawbacks. A public commitment to assign revenues from an environmental product tax to an environmental clean-up fund or another environmental purpose can strengthen support for environmental product taxation both from voters and from businesses. A more complex package of measures could combine the introduction of environmentally related product taxes with spending measures financed by some of the revenue generated, with the aim of increasing the scale of consumer response. A good example of this in OECD countries has been public spending to promote efficiency investments in order to increase the responsiveness of energy consumption to higher energy prices.

On the other hand, there are well-known reasons to limit the extent of revenue earmarking. Although revenue earmarking to environmental funds has been quite widespread, very few other taxes are earmarked in this way, for good reasons. Assigning revenues of a tax to a particular budget line risks long-term inefficiency and rigidity in the allocation of public spending, as spending programmes linked to buoyant revenue sources grow at the expense of those funded from taxes with less-buoyant revenues. These changes can be arbitrary and inefficient. If an environmental tax reduces the consumption of a particular "dirty" good, revenues accruing to the corresponding environmental budget fall automatically, while the need for public environmental spending is not necessarily reduced.

There are significant benefits from allowing revenues from environmentally related taxes to contribute to the general public budget. Additional revenues from environmental product taxes may allow the government to reduce other taxes (on labour or investment) and/or lower public borrowing and/or increase public spending. In some OECD countries this has been a powerful way of gathering public support for environmental taxes. In Sweden and in the UK, for example, some environmental taxes have been introduced along with an explicit public commitment to use the revenues to reduce income taxes or payroll taxes paid by employers.

3.4 Legal and institutional issues

3.4.1 Inter-departmental co-operation in policy development and implementation

Countries differ in how they divide responsibility between different ministries or government departments. In most countries, however, the successful introduction of environmental product tax policies has required co-ordination and co-operation between two separate branches of government:

- Environment ministries, responsible for policies to protect the environment from pollution and other forms of damage; and
- Ministries of finance, responsible for the design of the tax system, for policy decisions about tax rates and revenues, and, in most countries, for the management or oversight of the revenue collection agency responsible for the day-to-day operation of the tax system.

In most countries that have introduced successful and well-functioning environmentally related product taxes, the development of these taxes and their subsequent implementation has required co-ordination between the environment ministry and the ministry of finance. The involvement of the environment ministry is needed to ensure that the taxes have a clear environmental logic. The ministry of finance needs to be involved to ensure that the taxes are compatible with the rest of the tax system and make full use of the experience and resources of the existing tax administration. With respect to imported goods, these functions are usually carried out by the customs service. In addition, the ministry of economy is usually responsible for strategic planning and analysis of the impact of taxes on resource efficiency and key economic indicators.

The first step in effective policy development in this area is to establish the procedure for this crucial co-ordination. This may take the form of an inter-ministerial task force or a similar mechanism to develop a joint policy proposal and implementation plan.

The extent and nature of the inter-departmental discussion and co-operation on policy development and implementation needs to reflect the tax design option that has been chosen, whether or not to integrate environmental product taxes into the existing structure of VAT. But whatever decision is taken about the implementation mechanism, there are important gains to be made from co-ordination and co-operation between agencies, and even a wholly-separate environmental product tax mechanism would be able to benefit from extensive points of contact and information exchange with the existing fiscal administration.

The cross-ministry perspective is also useful in developing an effective and well-coordinated response to the concerns about competitiveness and the household tax burden that have often been raised in public discussion of proposals for environmentally-related product taxes. These issues are discussed in more detail in Sections 3.5 and 3.6.

Various forms of stakeholder consultation may be required in the course of developing a policy proposal and legislation. Different countries have different practices regarding the extent of consultation with industries (via business associations) that may be affected by proposed legislation. Generally speaking, the consultation procedure should ensure that policy development is better informed about the cost implications for businesses. At the same time, it opens opportunities for aggressive lobbying by firms which may compromise the environmental and revenue-raising effectiveness of the instrument. More extensive consultation may be needed if the decision is taken to develop a stand-alone system of tax administration for the environmental product taxes.

The experience of OECD countries suggests that meaningful inter-departmental co-operation put in place at an early stage greatly improves the functionality and political sustainability of environmentally related product taxes.

3.4.2 Longer-term institutional issues

In addition to the need for inter-agency co-ordination in the process of policy development, there are some important longer-term issues concerning the institutional location of responsibility for rate-setting and for future policy development.

Assigning the responsibility for setting and modifying environmentally related tax rates is an important factor of the system's long-run effectiveness. If the decisions are made by the ministry of finance alone, and the revenue accrues to the general public budget, there may be a risk that revenue considerations will dominate policy choices at the expense of environmental effectiveness. A similar risk could arise if the tax rate decisions are made by the environment ministry and the revenues accrue to an environmental fund it manages. Since the environment ministry may have relatively few revenue sources, there is a danger that revenue rather than environmental considerations will dominate its decision-making about the tax rates.

There is no simple institutional assignment that will ensure that an appropriate balance will always be drawn between revenue and environmental considerations, or indeed that wider considerations such as those relating to taxpayer burdens are given appropriate weight. However, defining clear principles for setting the tax rates based on their environmental rationale may guard against the taxes being used solely for revenue-raising without regard for environmental effectiveness.

3.4.3 Institutional issues and the achievement of policy stability

Stability in tax rates is important if the system is not to be disruptive to business and ineffective in achieving its environmental goals. Frequent change will alter the incentive to produce greener products. Firms may need to make substantial investments in order to switch to producing greener products, and they are unlikely to make these investments unless they are confident that the incentives provided by product taxes will be maintained consistently over time.

This suggests that considerable attention should be paid to institutional arrangements for enhancing stability in product taxes:

- An important starting point for stability is to ensure that the introduction of product taxes is based on cross-party consensus, rather than partisan controversy.
- Stability is more likely if the initial legislation is realistic rather than overly ambitious about the tax rate. A very high initial tax rate may encourage political opposition and policy reversal.
- Stability requires policy-makers to avoid frequent minor adjustments which cause costly disruption without any real benefit. One possible strategy to discourage "tinkering" is to pre-announce an intended time path for the tax rate as a guide to future policy decisions. While it is not possible to guarantee future finance ministry decisions, announcing a long-term strategy for the tax rate may help to emphasise that these taxes are different from conventional taxes directed only at revenue-raising.

3.5 Addressing competitiveness concerns

Most OECD countries that have introduced environmentally related product taxes have found that the announcement of these measures has prompted concerns about their potential adverse impact on the competitiveness of domestic producers, and hence on national output and employment.

These concerns have been particularly vocal where the taxes apply to products used as inputs to production. Proposals to increase taxes on industrial energy use and on motor fuel, in particular, have sparked heated debate about the effects on national producers and employment. In the case of taxes on the carbon content of fuels, introduced to reduce greenhouse gas emissions, there have been concerns that not only would national producers be disadvantaged in comparison with producers abroad who did not have to bear such taxes, but also that the loss of competitiveness of national producers would cause "carbon leakage" to production locations abroad, which would offset any benefits from the domestic emissions reduction.

With the exception of fuels, however, most of the focus of environmentally related product taxes in OECD countries has been on consumer products, which raise much less concerns about adverse competitiveness effects. In principle, any such taxes should apply equally to the sale of all products of a particular sort, whether domestically-produced or imported. While there might be some reduction in the overall market for the taxed "dirty" products, this effect is likely to be relatively modest compared with the dramatic changes in output that could arise if imports and domestic production were treated differently.

Even though the overall effects on the competitiveness of domestic firms may be modest, some significant lobbying should be anticipated, especially if some national firms focus their production particularly on the "dirty" products that will be adversely affected by the product tax. If the objective is to improve the environment by reducing consumption of these products, there may be little that should be done to respond positively to the concerns of the firms affected. It will be important to ensure that the measure is not watered down to the point where it is ineffective.

It is also important that policy instruments such as environmentally related product taxes not be subverted by industrial pressures to advance the interests of particular producers. A firm that succeeds in having its "dirty" products exempted from an environmental product tax while the full tax is borne by its equally "dirty" competitors will gain significant business advantage and additional profits. The prospect of these profits may well justify the firm's self-interested lobbying to secure such tax advantage. Policy-makers need to be aware of this risk and mount an effective defence of the product tax policy against unjustified lobbying.

One tactic to counter business lobbying to secure exemptions and other unjustified tax privileges is to commission an objective assessment of the environmental case for the tax and to justify the products that are to be included within the scope of the tax on the basis of clear environmental criteria. The tax is much more likely to be defensible against erosion if the products included have been selected on the basis of clear criteria applied systematically across all competing products than if the selection of products has been arbitrary.

Another defence against self-interested business lobbying is public support for the proposed measure. Transparency in discussion about the reasons for the reform may help to build wider public understanding and support for the tax measure. Well-publicised earmarking of revenues for some environmental purpose may also help to consolidate public support and reduce vulnerability to lobbying.

Packaging the tax with explicit reductions of other taxes may be an alternative strategy. A number of countries have been able to introduce quite significant environmentally related taxes in this way. In the UK, for example, a number of environmental tax measures intended to have incentive effects have been introduced on a revenue-neutral basis, with the additional tax collected on the "dirty" activity being used to finance a cut in the payroll tax paid by employers. Not all firms gain equally from the use of the revenue in this way, but it does create gainers as well as losers. Some firms that stand to gain from quite significant tax reductions may provide a counter-weight to the lobbying of the firms which stand to lose.

3.6 Addressing income distribution concerns

Some proposals for environmental product taxes have prompted concerns about the impact on poorer households. The main focus of these concerns has, again, been the taxation of energy, and in particular the taxation of household energy supply for heating, lighting and other household consumption. In some countries, both in the OECD area and among transitional and developing economies, household energy spending is a high percentage of poorer households' incomes, so additional taxes on household energy constitute a much higher proportion of household incomes among the poor than among the rich.

Although the taxation of household energy consumption results in a heavier additional tax burden for poor households, the additional tax paid, in money terms, is bigger for households with higher incomes (because they use more energy). The revenue generated can be used in a number of ways, depending on political and policy judgments, to compensate poorer households for the additional energy tax they would pay, including:

- Paying higher pensions and social benefits to poorer households;
- Paying for energy efficiency improvements in poorer households – better insulation, buying fuel-efficient appliances, etc.; and
- Reducing other taxes, in particular those which already bear heavily on poorer households.

There are few, if any, other commodities where environmental product taxes raise any real distributional concerns. Most products, apart from energy, that have been subject to environmental product taxes are either products consumed disproportionately by the rich, such as motor vehicles, or are small items in most household budgets, such as batteries, disposable cameras, etc.

References

EC (2012), *Use of economic instruments and waste management performances*, Final Report, 10 April 2012, http://ec.europa.eu/environment/waste/pdf/final_report_10042012.pdf.

EC (2008), *The Use of Differential VAT Rates to Promote Changes in Consumption and Innovation*, 25 June 2008, http://ec.europa.eu/environment/enveco/taxation/pdf/vat_final.pdf.

EC (2001), *Commission Communication on Tax policy in the European Union – Priorities for the years ahead (COM(2001) 260 final)*, European Commission.

EU (2004), *Council Directive 2003/96/EC of 27 October 2003 restructuring the Community framework for the taxation of energy products and electricity*, European Commission.

Fullerton, D., A. Leicester and S. Smith (2010), "*Environmental Taxes*", in J. Mirrlees et al, (eds.), Dimensions of Tax Design: the Mirrlees Review, Oxford University Press, www.ifs.org.uk/mirrleesreview/dimensions/ch5.pdf

Hogg, D. et al. (2014), *Study on Environmental Fiscal Reform Potential in 12 EU Member States,* Final Report to DG Environment of the European Commission, Eunomia Research and Consulting and Aarhus University, http://ec.europa.eu/environment/integration/green_semester/pdf/EFR-Final%20Report.pdf

OECD (2013), *Taxing Energy Use: A Graphical Analysis*, OECD Publishing, Paris, http://dx.doi.org/10.1787/9789264183933-en.

OECD (2011), *Taxation, innovation and the environment: A policy brief*, www.oecd.org/environment/tools-evaluation/48178034.pdf.

OECD (2010), *Taxation, innovation and the environment*, OECD Publishing, Paris, http://dx.doi.org/10.1787/9789264087637-en.

OECD (2009), *The scope for CO_2-based differentiation in motor vehicle taxes*, OECD, Paris.

OECD (2007), *Instrument mixes for environmental policy*, OECD Publishing, Paris, http://dx.doi.org/10.1787/9789264018419-en.

OECD (2006), *The Political Economy of Environmentally Related Taxes*, OECD Publishing, Paris, http://dx.doi.org/10.1787/9789264025530-en.

OECD (1999), *Improving the environment through reducing subsidies*, OECD Publishing, Paris, http://dx.doi.org/10.1787/9789264162679-en.

OECD (1993), *Taxation and the environment: Complementary policies*, OECD, Paris.

Pavel, J. and L. Vítek (2012), "*Transaction costs of environmental taxation: the administrative burden*", in J. Milne and M.S. Andersen (eds.), Handbook of research on environmental taxation, Cheltenham: Edward Elgar.

Vollebergh, H. (2012), *Environmental taxes and green growth: Exploring possibilities within energy and climate policy*, PBL Netherlands Environmental Assessment Agency, The Hague.

4. Deposit-refund systems: Design and implementation

Deposit-refund systems (DRS) can be employed to ensure high rates of recovery of certain tightly defined and specific products, where the mechanism of charging deposits and paying refunds can be operated at an acceptable cost relative to the gains from achieving high rates of return of the products concerned. However, despite the relative simplicity of the concept, implementation of a DRS may involve considerable complexity and high costs of operation which may act as a burden on producers, distributors or retailers. This section discusses key decisions and practical steps to be taken in introducing a DRS, such as commodity coverage, the choice between a single-producer and a common industry-wide scheme, treatment of smaller producers and importers, setting the level of the deposit, and the need for government intervention in a DRS.

4.1 Incentives for behavioural change

Deposit-refund systems aim at changing consumers' behaviour by incentivising the return of product packaging or end-of-life products. Typically, legislation establishing a DRS mandates specific actions on the part of producers and retailers, and may set up new institutions to handle the collection and processing of returned products. Apart from ensuring compliance with these requirements, deposit-refund systems do not generally seek to stimulate significant behavioural change on the part of producers.

DRS can be used very effectively to ensure high rates of recovery for certain categories of packaging and end-of-life products:

- End-of-life products or packaging to be collected for re-use or recycling (such as bottles, cans and other drinks containers);
- Products or materials that would be hazardous or excessively costly if discarded in the general waste stream, to be collected for specialist safe disposal (e.g. batteries or waste motor oil); and
- Products containing valuable materials to be re-used or recovered.

Public policy generally needs to address only the first two of these three categories. If manufacturers of printer cartridges or other sophisticated and costly products wish to recover used items for re-use on a commercial basis, there is no need for legislation to regulate the operation of their deposit-refund arrangements. There is a need for policy intervention only where there is an important and identified reason for separate recovery of items that would not otherwise happen on a commercial basis.

The mechanism involved in a DRS is generally straightforward. For example, a deposit is charged by the seller when a battery is sold, and then refunded when the used battery is returned to an approved collection point. High rates of return for re-use or recycling can be achieved because the refund provides consumers with an incentive to return items through appropriate channels rather than discarding them in general waste.

However, despite the relative simplicity of the concept, implementation of a DRS may involve considerable complexity and high operational costs which may act as a burden on producers, distributors or retailers. Some or all of these costs may then be passed on to consumers in higher product prices, resulting in a burden on consumers that needs to be weighed carefully against the system's aspired benefits. If the costs of operating a DRS are very high, this could encourage producers, retailers or consumers to shift towards packaging or products that lie outside the scope of the system, which tends to encourage imported products at the expense of locally-produced products.

The key issues relating to policy design and practical implementation that need to be addressed in the introduction of a deposit-refund system are the following:

- The scope, in terms of products to be covered;
- Institutional arrangements, in particular the choice between producer-based and industry-based DRS;
- Setting the rate of deposit and refund, which governs consumer behaviour and return rates; and
- Arrangements for monitoring and enforcing compliance.

4.2 Design issues

4.2.1 Commodity coverage

Deposit-refund systems need to be applied to tightly defined categories of products so that it is clear which products the deposit would be charged on, and so that refunds are paid only for products where the deposit had previously been levied at the appropriate rate. The refund arrangements are usually operated by individuals collecting the returned items, so it needs to be clear to them which items are eligible for a refund. It should be possible to identify items eligible for refund quickly through visual inspection or by some prominent and distinctive marking on the product. This issue is important not only for the smooth functioning of the product return arrangements, but also for the financial control and prevention of fraud within the retail sector.

In practice, successful DRS have been implemented for drinks containers such as glass bottles, cans and cartons. Some countries have been able to specify other products on which a deposit should be paid and subsequently refunded, e.g. batteries and motor vehicles. In each case, these are easily identifiable commodities, with little doubt whether a particular item lies within the scope of the system of outside it.

However, it is ***not*** possible to operate a satisfactory DRS on the following types of products:

- Products that have "blurred boundaries" – in other words, where the definition of the item is vague, as for example "packaging", or where the definition reflects characteristics which are a matter of judgement, such as "green" or "sustainable" products.
- Products that cannot be identified by simple visual inspection. This rules out, for example, a DRS for batteries of a particular type (e.g. nickel-cadmium batteries), unless the batteries can be easily distinguished from other types not subject to the system through clear and distinctive marking, as has been done in Denmark (Section 2.2).
- Products of some producers but not others, unless products within the scope of the system can be clearly and distinctively marked in a way that that has effective legal protection. (A distinctive logo could be used to mark products within the system, but legislation would be required to prohibit producers outside the system from using the logo, and resources would need to be devoted to ensuring effective enforcement of this.)
- Products that can be reconfigured or sub-divided so as to increase the number of refunds to be paid.

4.2.2 Single-producer or common industry-wide scheme?

A key policy choice in designing a DRS concerns the balance between individual and collective responsibility that the scheme will impose on producers. Deposit-refund systems can be operated separately by each producer or entirely or partially by the industrial sector.

Producer-based DRS

A system operated by individual producers would require, for example, battery producer A to levy a deposit on the batteries it sells, and then to collect its own batteries, returning the deposits which had previously been paid by its own customers. Producer B would likewise charge a deposit on its batteries and refund the deposit on those of its batteries that are returned. Each producer would be required to operate a similar DRS, but the systems would operate independently. Each producer would face targets for the percentage of its products that it should recover, and would be liable for penalties if it failed to operate the required scheme or to achieve the required rate of recovery.

A producer-based DRS imposes unambiguous and straightforward obligations on individual producers. However, it can be complicated for consumers, who may have to return similar products to a range of different collection points, depending on their manufacturer, which may lead to lower rates of return than in a simpler scheme.

Industry-based DRS

Under a collective industry-wide scheme, all producers of a particular product would charge the same deposit and would then be required to make refunds to all items returned to them, regardless of the original producer. An industry-based DRS is often used to recover single-use packaging for recycling. If an industry-based system is to be employed for items which are to be re-used, such as beer bottles, for example, these would need to be of a common design.

An industry-based DRS is less complex for consumers, who have a wider choice of collection points and who do not need to concern themselves with finding a collection point that will take the products of a particular manufacturer.

In practice, manufacturers rarely make sales directly to the public. Most sales are made through retail outlets, and these may handle the products of more than one producer. If deposit-refund arrangements are organised separately by each producer, retailers may need to collect, store and make arrangements to return items to each producer, and to keep separate accounts of the deposits returned on each producer's items, making the system's operation exceedingly complex. A collective industry-wide scheme is much easier for retail outlets to operate and involves less bureaucracy and lower storage requirements.

Recent technological changes have made it possible to automate many of the processes involved in collecting drinks containers, making refunds, and accounting for quantities collected and payments. Some designs of "reverse vending machine" are able to handle many different designs of drinks container and to make different refunds for different items. The costs of reverse vending machines will, however, only be warranted in locations where large numbers of items are being collected, which creates a reason to try and reduce the number of collection points, so as to be able to make the maximum use of automation. A further implication of the these technological advances is that they reduce the need for easy-to-operate systems and make it possible to operate with much more complicated deposit and refund arrangements compared to the manual processing of refunds by small-scale shops and other outlets.

Most deposit-refund systems need to accommodate considerable asymmetry between the pattern of deposits collected and refunds paid out, especially where a single industry-wide scheme is in operation. Since customers can return items to *any* retail outlet, and not just the retailers selling the brand they purchased, customers may choose to return items to the retail outlet that is most convenient to them, even though they may have initially bought the product elsewhere. Retailers in residential areas or those with good car parking facilities might be expected to collect more items than they had originally sold.

Some arrangements are needed to ensure that appropriate deposit income is transferred to the locations making higher levels of refunds. It cannot be simply assumed that their costs of collection will be covered by the price they charged for the initial sale, because the sale was made by someone else.

4.2.3 Treatment of smaller producers and importers

The costs of operating a producer-based deposit-refund scheme are a disproportionate burden on firms with a small volume of sales, especially if it is spread over a large number of retailers. Such producers will need to make arrangements to collect returned products (e.g. bottles) from all of the retailers through whom their products are sold, but will not gain the economies of scale which are available to producers with a higher volume of sales. The result is that the cost of operating the DRS will be higher per unit sold for small producers, which will either reduce their profitability compared to larger producers or make their products less attractive for retailers to stock. A producer-based DRS can thus act as a barrier to market entry for small firms and can give an undesirable competitive advantage to large firms, which can spread the costs of the DRS over many more units sold. By contrast, small-scale producers could participate in an industry-based DRS on a more or less equal footing with their larger competitors.

Since many importers typically are selling premium or niche brands with small market share, importers tend to be disadvantaged relative to large domestic producers under a producer-based DRS. However, small-scale importers are also at a disadvantage under an industry-wide DRS, if this imposes requirements for uniform product packaging (e.g. a standard bottle design or a label with a distinctive logo) that differs from the packaging or labelling used when selling the same product in other markets. Importers would then need to produce products in the required product packaging in order to sell in this particular market, which will add to their costs of production.

4.2.4 Setting the level of the deposit

In a conventional DRS, a fixed deposit is charged when the product is sold (e.g. 10 cents per bottle). When the product or its container is later returned, an amount equal to the deposit is refunded to the individual making the return. If all items sold are later returned for refund, all the money collected in deposits is later returned through refunds.

A crucial policy decision to be made in introducing a DRS concerns the level at which the deposit and refund should be set. The amount refunded for each item returned is the key element in the system which governs consumer behaviour and hence the likely effectiveness of the system in achieving a high rate of return. The following factors should be taken into consideration in setting the level of deposit and refund:

- ***Achieving a high return rate***. The higher the amount of the deposit and refund, the stronger the incentive for consumers to return the product for refund. Efficient operation of a DRS requires that a high percentage of products be returned in order to justify incurring the high fixed costs of the separate collection arrangements. This is particularly important when the DRS seeks to ensure the return of hazardous items. It is difficult to make an accurate forecast of the rate of return that will be achieved by any given deposit/refund level, but international experience provides a useful benchmark, and the legislation needs to provide scope for the deposit and refund rates to be adjusted in the light of the return rates achieved.

- ***Costs of non-return***. If the deposit and refund are set at a low level, the incentive for consumers to return items will be low, and many may be discarded in the general waste stream or elsewhere. This implies that a second consideration in setting the rate of the deposit/refund should be the costs that would be incurred if the product were not returned for refund. With a glass bottle, for example, this would include the higher cost of replacing the bottle with a new one than re-using the returned bottle, plus the waste management costs of collecting bottles in the general waste stream and/or the environmental damage caused if the bottle is discarded as litter. The refund should be set at least as high as the total of these costs incurred if the bottle was not returned.
- ***Balancing financial effects on firms***. With an industry-based scheme, it is important that the scheme not confer disproportionate benefits on producers who happen to receive a high share of returned items, nor should it impose disproportionate costs on them. Some producers will find that they get more bottles back than others, and if the refund they have to pay for each bottle is significantly lower than the value of the bottles, this would create a significant benefit for them. Equally, if the refund greatly exceeds the value of the bottles, producers might be tempted to discourage consumers from returning bottles to them. Setting the refund at a level roughly equal to the value of recovered items to the producer would tend to avoid disputes between firms about unfair benefits to some participants from the system's operation.
- ***Avoiding complexity***. It is desirable to avoid unnecessary complexity in the structure of deposit and refund rates. While it may be tempting to propose a sophisticated tariff structure, there are practical reasons for simplicity. For example, a single rate per glass bottle is much easier to operate than multiple rates for different sizes of bottles.
- ***Inflation provision***. An important issue in setting deposit and refund rates is covering the effect of inflation. If the scheme aims at maintaining the incentive for the return of bottles, the rates of deposit and refund must be increased periodically, in line with the inflation. Whenever the rates of deposit and refund are increased, it is inevitable that some returns will receive a refund which differs from the deposit previously charged. More important than the brief unfairness of giving some consumers refunds that are higher than the deposit they paid is the danger that the uprating of deposit and refund rates creates incentives for speculative hoarding of items in anticipation of higher refund rates. This is potentially disruptive to the logistics of the collection and waste management operations and particularly costly for firms relying on the returned items for re-use. From this perspective, frequent adjustment of the refund rate in small steps in line with inflation is better than occasional large changes which would allow hoarders to make substantial profits.

4.3 Legal and institutional issues

The requirements for legislation for DRS depend on the underlying reason for introducing the DRS. Where DRS is being used to manage items which generate hazardous wastes; the need for legislation and procedures for compliance monitoring is much more extensive than in other cases (Table 4.1.).

Deposit-refund systems to collect items of significant value for re-use or materials recovery could be introduced by firms on a purely commercial basis. Such commercial arrangements require no legislative underpinning or public policy intervention. However, legislation is normally required to underpin a DRS introduced to achieve waste management policy objectives – either to achieve high rates of recycling or to ensure a high rate of recovery of items or materials which would be hazardous within the waste stream. The costs of operating a DRS are likely to be substantial for the producers and retailers involved, and legislation will then be needed to establish which firms are covered by the requirement to operate a DRS, what their obligations are, what performance targets they are required to meet, and what sanctions will be applied for non-compliance.

Table 4.1. Need for government intervention in DRS

	DRS to recover items of value	DRS for waste management	DRS for managing hazardous items
Purpose of DRS	Save resources by re-using collected items	Prevent littering; enable higher rate of re-use and recycling	Ensure safe disposal
Examples of products	Beer bottles, computer print cartridges	Single-use drinks containers	Batteries
Need for legislation	No, if recovered value exceeds operating costs of DRS	Legislation essential to institute a DRS, but not necessarily to specify subsequent treatment of collected items	Legislation needed to establish a DRS and to govern disposal practices for hazardous materials collected
Enforcement and monitoring required	Little or none	Monitoring of deposits and collection	Monitoring of collection and subsequent disposal
Need for public financial support	Negligible: participants benefit from recovery.	Low, as long as the system covers all relevant firms. Some subsidy may be needed to avoid "unfair" burdens on smaller firms.	Public importance of safe collection and disposal may justify public funding of subsidy for return, which could exceed initial deposit.

Where a DRS is to be operated on an industry-wide basis, with firms collecting items that had been produced and sold by other firms, the legislation will need to establish a central co-ordinating institution for the system. This could take the form of an industry-owned non-profit organisation (a model which has been employed successfully in many of the European countries that have introduced deposit-refund systems for single-use drinks containers). Alternatively, the role of co-ordinating institution could be performed by a public agency. The key tasks of the co-ordinating institution would be:

- To establish the operating rules of the system (product coverage, marking of products to show deposits paid, obligations on firms to take back, etc.);
- To require firms to account for deposits collected and refunds made and to make appropriate financial transfers between firms to compensate possible imbalances between deposit revenues and refund payments; and
- To monitor compliance by firms with the system's requirements, particularly to avoid systematic fraud.

The costs of a central co-ordinating institution could either be borne by the public sector or shared between participating firms, with contributions to the operating costs levied on firms in proportion to the value of sales, the volume of production or some other appropriate formula.

It is possible that negotiated agreements between the public authorities and industry representatives may be sufficient to establish and maintain well-functioning deposit-refund arrangements for certain products without the need for formal legislation. The threat of legislation may be sufficient to induce industry representatives to agree to implement a scheme on a voluntary basis. They may, for example, fear that legislation would impose a more inflexible system, with higher costs, more bureaucratic audit, or the threat of onerous penalty regimes for non-compliance.

International practice includes a number of examples where deposit-refund systems (and EPR schemes) have been introduced on a voluntary basis by industry bodies. It is clear that the threat of onerous legislation can be a strong motivation for members of an industry organisation to agree to co-operate on a collective voluntary system. However, the experience of such agreements also indicates that there is a risk that such schemes may deliver less than they promise once the pressure for legislation has subsided. This danger can be reduced if the voluntary commitment is sufficiently clear and concrete about what practical arrangements will be put in place and what quantitative targets will be achieved. This creates a realistic opportunity to monitor compliance with the agreement and, if the agreement proves to be ineffective, to justify the introduction of legislation.

References

Bohm, P. (1981), *Deposit-Refund Systems: Theory and Applications to Environmental, Conservation, and Consumer Policy*, Johns Hopkins University Press.

Tasaki, T., Numata, D. and Tojo, N. (2010), *Survey of deposit-refund systems in non-Japanese countries*, National Institute for Environmental Studies, Tsukuba.

5. Extended Producer Responsibility: Design and implementation

A frequent objective of Extended Producer Responsibility (EPR) schemes is to ensure secure and safe collection and disposal of substances or products that would otherwise be hazardous or harmful within the general waste stream. Another frequent motivation is to reduce public waste management costs by shifting the burden of collecting and managing significant parts of the waste stream away from tax-financed municipal operations. This section discusses commodity coverage of EPR schemes as well as issues of design, constitution and financing of Producer Responsibility Organisations (PROs). It also addresses the establishment and enforcement of EPR performance targets as well as costs borne by industry and consumers.

5.1 Incentives for behavioural change

Like deposit-refund systems, most EPR policies aim to encourage separate collection of products to permit cost-effective re-use, or higher rates of recycling or materials recovery. A frequent objective of EPR schemes is to ensure secure and safe collection and disposal of products that would otherwise be hazardous or harmful within the general waste stream. An additional motivation is often to reduce public waste management costs by shifting the burden of managing significant parts of the waste stream away from tax-financed municipal operations.

Some EPR schemes have a more ambitious objective, to stimulate the production and sale of "greener" products with lower end-of-life disposal costs. In principle, when producers are made responsible for these costs, they have a reason to take them into account in product design and manufacture. However, it is difficult to design a practical scheme that achieves this effect without excessive complexity. For firms to face a meaningful incentive for waste-reducing innovation in product design, the costs borne by each producer participating in the scheme would need to be very accurately related to the waste management costs generated by its ***own*** products. Most schemes in international practice involve simple cost-sharing rules between firms, and these do not provide strong incentives for waste-reducing product innovation.

Unlike deposit-refund systems, EPR typically leaves producers, either individually or collectively, with more flexibility to determine how they achieve the objectives of the policy. This flexibility can reduce the burden on producers, but it also means there is a greater risk that the policy could fail to achieve the intended outcomes. For this reason, it is essential that policy design start from a clear assessment of the objectives of the policy and the elements needed to ensure their achievement.

5.2 Design issues

EPR schemes vary, but the following features are common to many schemes:

- Producers are assigned certain obligations concerning the collection ("take-back") of product packaging or end-of-life products, either at the level of individual firms or, more commonly, through one or more industry-sponsored collective agencies (Producer Responsibility Organisations or PROs);
- Producers are required to bear the costs of collection, recycling and waste management of the collected products and materials, either individually or by sharing the operating costs of a collective PRO;
- Rules or targets are set either for individual firms or for the collective PRO, governing the methods of waste management of recovered products and/or specifying minimum required rates of re-use or recycling.

5.2.1 Commodity coverage

EPR can be introduced for individual products or for a whole category of products manufactured by a particular industrial sector. No country has introduced legislation imposing EPR obligations across the whole of manufacturing and retail business, and there would be major practical difficulties in doing so.

Examples of EPR applying to individual products are seen in many countries. The products to which EPR has been successfully applied are much more varied than those subject to deposit-refund systems. Many countries have more than one EPR scheme, each of them designed to meet particular objectives relevant to the product concerned. Thus, for example, the purpose of an EPR scheme for batteries or for waste oil may be primarily to ensure that hazardous materials do not enter the general waste stream, while a scheme for used car tyres may aim to reduce the hazard of fires in large-scale tyre dumps, and a scheme for packaging waste may be primarily concerned with promoting reductions in the quantity of such waste.

It is desirable to focus EPR on a tightly-defined product or product group. This ensures that the number of firms involved is manageable and that the scheme can be designed in the best way to achieve the specific objectives relevant to that product.

Different objectives typically require different organisation and operating rules. Where the aim is to prevent hazardous materials entering the waste stream, a high priority should be given to ensuring a high level of participation and to monitoring and enforcement. Some public funding may be desirable to ensure that incentives for non-participation are low. On the other hand, where the aim is incentivising waste reductions, the most important element in the scheme is the financial burden placed on participants, as this is what will encourage waste reductions.

Nevertheless, even where separate EPR schemes are introduced for different products, there may be advantages in introducing various common elements in design and operation. It may be possible for a number of schemes to be covered by a single piece of legislation, reducing the risk that the effectiveness of the scheme could be undermined by lobbying by an individual firm or industry. Common design also makes implementation easier, and those involved in each scheme can see other examples in operation, providing benchmarks against which performance can be judged.

5.2.2 Producer Responsibility Organisation

Most of the wide range of EPR schemes that have been implemented across OECD countries do not require individual firms to directly manage their own end-of-life waste products, but instead assign this role to a Producer Responsibility Organisation, which frequently is a not-for-profit firm owned and run by industry. The PRO may collect and process end-of-life products from retailers who have collected them from consumers, through its own network of collection points. Alternatively, the PRO may subcontract collection to municipal services and then handle the waste management, either directly, through its own sorting, dismantling and recycling activities, or by contracting with specialist waste management and recycling firms.

In principle, PROs could take a number of institutional forms:

- A private non-profit company, owned by an industry body, by firms or by a public agency;
- A private profit-making company, with individual or corporate shareholders; or
- A public agency. If the PRO takes the form of a public agency, it is particularly important that its operating rules require it to operate on a non-subsidised basis, covering its operating costs from the revenues it obtains from firms.

PRO "membership"

There are different schemes concerning the rules for participation in the PRO. In some schemes, a single PRO is established, and all collection and waste management activities are required to be channelled through this organisation. In other schemes, firms may have the option of opting out of the PRO and conducting the take-back and recycling activities individually. In other cases, more than one PRO may be established, competing for business from individual firms.

In some countries that have employed EPR, the design and operating constitution of the PRO has been specified through legislation. In others, the PRO has been established on a negotiated voluntary basis through discussion between public authorities and the relevant industry organisation. How far the latter route is practicable will depend, amongst other factors, on the existence of an industry organisation capable of making long-term commitments on behalf of its members. There are significant risks of "free riding" in any scheme of EPR involving an element of voluntary action by firms, because EPR is generally costly for firms, and a firm that neglects its obligations will gain advantage relative to its competitors (thereby undermining the effectiveness of the scheme).

The most efficient organisation of collection and recycling activities within a sector may take some time to emerge. The competitive pressure that arises when firms have the option of leaving existing bodies and setting up new arrangements will be an important part of the process of innovation and market adjustment, and EPR schemes should offer the maximum possible scope for this – consistent with adequate monitoring and compliance. However, it is important that a scheme start with workable structures capable of achieving the initial objectives and covering the products of all firms within the sector. The most effective way to do this may be for EPR legislation to include provisions to set up an initial PRO, to which all firms would initially be required to subscribe. This would become the "default" PRO within the scheme and may, for a time, be the only operator of collection and recycling. Over time, a more diverse range of PROs – and, possibly, single-firm collection and recycling operations – may emerge, leading to greater efficiency.

There are some important conditions for this process of institutional development to contribute to greater efficiency. One is that all PROs, and any opt-outs based on single-firm collection and recycling operations, should be subject to equivalent targets and effective monitoring of compliance, with meaningful sanctions for non-compliance. "Opting out" should not offer an opportunity for non-compliance. A second key condition is that PROs should face equivalent financial conditions, based on cost-sharing by the participating firms. The initial PRO should not be given competitive advantage by public subsidy, nor should it be burdened with responsibilities that are more onerous than those applying to opt-out firms and alternative PROs.

Flexibility in operation

A key policy decision is how much flexibility to permit the PRO in the methods it uses to achieve the required amount of collection and recycling. The legislation may require the PRO to operate a DRS to recover items. This ensures that households have a clear financial incentive to return items to the appropriate collection point, but the arrangements for collecting deposits and subsequently returning them can be complicated and costly.

In some countries it has been demonstrated that significant rates of separation and recovery can be achieved even without providing households with a direct refund incentive. Separate return for recycling is often encouraged by forbidding the disposal of certain items within general household waste. PROs may also be able to achieve high rates of voluntary return through public education campaigns, and by ensuring that households can return items through convenient collection sites.

Leaving the PRO and its member firms to choose how to achieve the required outcomes may encourage desirable innovation and the adoption of lower-cost solutions. In some countries, PROs contract with municipalities to collect WEEE and other items on the PRO's behalf. Municipalities may be able to do this cheaper than the PRO itself by combining collection with regular collection of household garbage. The incentives for cost-saving efficiency are further enhanced in some countries by the presence of multiple PROs, which compete for members (i.e. for producers) by offering a more cost-effective achievement of the collection and recycling targets, and hence a lower subscription cost. In general, this efficiency-enhancing competition is highly desirable, but it needs to be backed up by rigorous public monitoring of compliance, to ensure that the competing PROs offer low charges through greater efficiency rather than through fraud or inadequate achievement of collection and recycling targets.

PRO financing

Typically, a PRO levies charges on participating firms to cover the net costs of its operation. The latter usually include costs of collection and subsequent treatment of waste products. Where the waste products are to be recycled, there may be significant costs of separation, sorting and transportation. In some cases, where commercially profitable recycling operations exist, the PRO may receive significant income from the sale of recyclable materials to recycling companies. In other cases, when recycling is required by the rules of the scheme but is not commercially viable, the PRO may need to pay to have recycling undertaken. The PRO will make a trading loss if its operating costs exceed any income received from recyclers, and this will need to be covered by contributions from members.

Financial contributions levied by a PRO to cover its net operating costs are usually proportional to the current and/or past sales volumes of participating firms. In some cases, the contributions include both a fixed amount, unrelated to market share, and a volume-related component. A fixed element in the charge levied on each firm may be justified if each additional firm imposes a significant additional cost on the PRO, regardless of its scale of activity, but it can impose a disproportionately heavy burden on small firms. The charge levied on firms could also be based on the characteristics of the products, especially those affecting waste management costs such as the use of composite materials that cannot be recycled. Then firms making "dirtier" products in terms of end-of-life waste management have to contribute more towards PRO costs for every unit sold than a firm making a product that is more easily recycled or re-used.

It is clear that these are crucial issues for individual firms participating in the PRO, in terms of both long-term environmental incentives and the impact of the EPR scheme on the pattern of competition within the industry. There are two key aspects:

- First, the incentives for a producer to design products that will have low waste management costs will be sharper if the waste management cost savings translate directly into lower contributions to the running costs of the PRO. If all firms share PRO costs equally, without regard to the waste management costs of their products, the incentive for an individual firm to make waste-reducing product changes may be small. Devising a scale of charges which reflects end-of-life waste costs for different products is difficult and potentially controversial between member firms. Nevertheless, it has been done in a number of cases in France, where, for example, charges for packaging materials have been differentiated to penalise material that is disruptive to the recycling process, and where charges for WEEE are levied according to the content of hazardous materials.

- Second, the competition within the industry may be affected by the relationship between PRO charges and product volumes. There are dangers in allowing the firms involved too much freedom to determine the rules of the PRO because dominant firms can use these rules to enhance their dominant position at the expense of new entrants and other competitors.

The practical arrangements for collecting the contributions from firms could take a number of forms, including:

- A public agency collecting contributions from firms and paying them over to the relevant PRO. This may have the advantage of using the tax authorities' enforcement information and powers.
- A public agency collecting and auditing firms' data on sales/imports of the product in question to ensure that the firms have provided honest data, and then supplying the PROs with information on the relative contribution they should levy on each of their members;
- An entirely PRO-run operation, in which the PRO requests information from each firm on its sales/imports, takes whatever measures it can to verify the accuracy of this information, and invoices each firm for its appropriate contribution. Since firms share the costs of the PRO, any shortfall in revenues due to dishonest reporting by one of its members is borne by the other members, who can exert pressure for accurate reporting, and have the option of leaving a PRO that is badly undermined by dishonesty.

The choice between these options should be judged on the basis of an assessment of what is most likely to work effectively in the given context.

Imported and "orphan" products

A PRO which collects and recycles all products of a specified type (e.g. batteries) will find that some of the products which it handles were not originally produced by its current members. These will include two major categories: imported products and "orphan" products, made by manufactures that have since gone out of business. It is generally desirable that the PRO accept these products from consumers on the same basis as others, especially if they would be hazardous if discarded in the general waste stream.

An EPR scheme can require large-scale commercial importers to contribute to the PRO on the same basis as domestic manufacturers and producers. However, it may be harder to ensure that smaller scale importers have any involvement in the PRO, especially when these are individuals purchasing foreign-made products either directly across the border or on internet sites. These are likely to be minor issues, but they can become a focus of considerable irritation for participating firms.

In some cases covering the costs of handling "orphan" products could become a problem. In some industries that have undergone major restructuring, a high proportion of current wastes may be the products of manufacturers who are no longer in business. These products, being older, may have relatively high waste management costs. Requiring existing producers to foot the bill for managing these wastes is likely to meet with a lot of opposition on the grounds that the burden is excessive and unjust. The best solution is probably some element of public subsidy to the operating costs of the PRO, based on the proportion of uncharged imported products and orphan products that it handles. This avoids the risk that a large bankruptcy or a sudden rise in imports will increase the contributions required from the PRO's member firms.

5.3 Legal and institutional issues

EPR legislation needs to specify the obligations which the EPR scheme will place on the relevant producers. These obligations usually cover end-of-life waste management, including disposal methods. EPR legislation should be clear and explicit, otherwise it may create uncertainty for business and lead to costly and wasteful litigation disputing the scope of application of the policy. In particular, it should specify the products covered by the scheme (as with deposit-refund systems) and the categories of firms subject to its requirements (only manufacturers or wholesale or retail firms involved in selling the product as well).

Firms covered by EPR obligations

In general, most schemes place the obligation on domestic producers and on importers. This ensures that someone is responsible for all sales made within the country concerned, and that only one firm is responsible for the end-of-life costs of each item sold. Some EPR schemes (especially those for packaging) share the responsibility among a number of market participants including producers, wholesalers and retailers, especially when it comes to financing its operation.

Shared responsibility in this way may be seen as "fair", and it may be a way of reducing the financial burden placed on any individual firm. It may also be a way of raising the awareness of all market participants of the costs of end-of-life waste management. However, it has the danger that it can blur and weaken responsibility, and hence reduce incentives for action, since no firm faces the full burden of responsibility for end-of-life costs. Whatever decision is made about firms to be covered by the obligations set up under the legislation, a choice will have to be made about how far this applies to firms with only a small involvement.

Nature of the obligations placed on firms

In some EPR schemes, the obligations for end-of-life costs are borne and carried out at the level of the individual producer. A firm may recover its own products and take responsibility – both physical and financial – for recycling and disposing of the wastes arising from its own products. Firms face individual targets and individual penalties if they fail to meet these targets.

If EPR is operated through an industry-wide PRO, the producers' primary responsibility is financial, and the targets and any penalties for non-compliance would apply to the PRO. Firms would share financial liability for non-compliance with the performance targets.

Targets or outcomes which firms are expected to achieve

One key aim of EPR is to ensure that producers manage the wastes from their end-of-life products in a way that contributes to higher environmental standards. The legislation, therefore, needs to contain a clear specification of the standards of waste management that producers are expected to achieve, either through individual management of their wastes or through the operations of the PRO which they finance and control. What proportion of their waste products should be collected through the EPR scheme, and what should then happen to the collected wastes? What proportion of the waste should be recycled?

The legislation may specify the targets directly or define a clear process for subsequent target-setting by the government. The latter option has the advantage that waste recovery and recycling targets can be adjusted more flexibly in the light of experience, though firms may fear that it increases the risks that they will face sudden and unrealistic demands to meet more stringent targets.

However the target is set, this is an important decision both for the environmental outcomes that the scheme will achieve and for the costs that EPR will impose on firms. The higher the rate of collection and the higher the rate of recycling required, the greater is likely to be the financial burden on firms.

Requirements for record-keeping, reporting and audit

Given the burden that EPR imposes on firms, it should not be expected that all firms will willingly comply with the requirements placed on them. EPR legislation should contain clear provisions for monitoring compliance so that firms that fail to meet their obligations can be clearly identified, and corrective action taken.

Both the public authorities and any collective industry-run PROs need to collect regular information on the performance of the scheme and on the relevant activities (sales, etc.) of individual participating firms. Both also need effective powers of audit and verification.

Mechanisms for enforcement action

EPR legislation also needs to specify the consequences for firms of failing to achieve the outcomes set in the legislation. An EPR scheme will only operate effectively with clear sanctions for non-compliance. In some countries, a significant part of the sanction for non-compliance is the potential reputational damage to firms which are seen to be failing to meet their obligations. However, a realistic judgement needs to be made about how much reliance can be placed on this as an incentive for compliance. The public authorities need to be able to apply appropriate sanctions for non-compliance, including financial penalties that are significantly higher than the potential profits that firms could make through non-compliance.

5.4 EPR performance targets and costs borne by industry and consumers

With a product tax, the crucial policy decision that governs the effectiveness of the scheme, and the costs imposed on producers and consumers, is a simple one – the choice of the rate of tax. Likewise, with a deposit-refund system, the effect is largely driven by the deposit rate that is set. With EPR, the crucial policy decisions that determine the effectiveness and the burdens borne by producers and consumers are less transparent but no less important. These decisions govern two aspects of the operation of the EPR scheme in particular:

- ***Collection rates:*** What is a realistic target to set for the percentage of the relevant waste stream to be recovered?

- ***Recycling and recovery rates:*** Should targets be set for the proportion of the collected waste to be recycled or for the percentage of materials recovery, and on what basis?

The higher is the target set for waste recovery, and the higher is the percentage of recovered items that must be recycled, the greater will be the operating cost of the scheme. A very high target for recovery risks requiring the PRO to incur high costs of collecting a relatively small number of additional units, probably well in excess of the social and environmental benefits of the additional recovery.

Where EPR obligations are imposed on individual firms, their costs of compliance will be most likely subsumed in the operating accounts of the company concerned and difficult to observe. Firms may assert that they bear excessive burdens in operating the scheme, but these claims will be almost impossible to verify. An EPR scheme run through a collective PRO offers, by contrast, greater scope for monitoring the costs of operation imposed on firms, since the turnover of the PRO, as measured in its accounts, is essentially the financial burden which firms must share. Institutional arrangements for EPR which require the PRO to produce and publish externally audited accounts provide a sound basis for assessing the burden placed on firms by EPR and for weighing this burden against the public benefits of safer disposal or recycling of the recovered materials.

The costs borne by consumers also need to be considered in assessing the overall cost of achieving waste management improvements through EPR. These consumer costs may include costs of separating items from the general waste stream and of transporting them to collection points. Very similar consumer costs are typically involved in the operation of deposit-refund systems, although an EPR scheme which aims to increase the rate of collection will need to seek innovative ways of reducing the costs to consumers of returning items. Ultimately, public understanding and support will be crucial to the successful operation of EPR. If consumers understand the reasons for EPR, they are more likely to be motivated to separate and return their waste products within the EPR scheme.

References

EC (2005), *Concerning issues of competition in waste management systems*, http://ec.europa.eu/competition/sectors/energy/waste_management.pdf.

Öko-Institut (2002), *The Green Dot and its benefits for the environment: life cycle analysis of scenarios for the future.* Report to DSD.

Porter, R. C. (2002), *The economics of waste*, Resources for the Future Press, Washington D.C.

Smith, S. (2005), *Analytical framework for evaluating the costs and benefits of extended producer responsibility programmes*, OECD, Paris.

Walls, M. (2006), *"EPR Policies and Product Design: Economic Theory and Selected Case Studies"*, paper prepared for OECD Working Group on Waste Prevention and Recycling, OECD, http://www.oecd.org/officialdocuments/publicdisplaydocumentpdf/?doclanguage=en&cote=env/epoc/wgwpr(2005)9/final.

Annex A. Development and implementation checklists

1. Environmentally related product taxes

Key initial policy decisions

- Identify priority areas where taxation could achieve a clear environmental benefit by reducing production or consumption of the taxed product.
- For environmental effectiveness, the tax or tax differentiation needs to apply to clearly identified products which are associated with environmental damage in the course of production or consumption, while not taxing alternative products which involve less environmental damage.
- Ensure that the level of environmental element in taxation is proportionate to the scale of environmental damage involved, and avoid introducing environmentally related taxes which are too low to change behaviour (i.e. the rate is less than 10% of the product's sales price).
- Determine where the revenues will be allocated. For environmental effectiveness it is not essential that the revenue from the taxes be earmarked to environmental expenditures.
- Prioritise the removal of environmentally-harmful subsidies before introducing environmental taxes
- Wherever possible, introduce environmental incentives into the structure of existing product taxes (such as fuel excises), since this will avoid the high costs of setting up and running new taxes.
- An early priority should be to establish institutional arrangements for co-operation in policy development and operation between the government departments and agencies responsible for the environment and those responsible for tax policy and operation.

Key legislative provisions

- Define the tax base (what is to be taxed?). Where practicable, implement environmentally related product taxes as an amount per unit or quantity, rather than as a percentage of selling price, since this will link the tax more closely to environmental damage.
- Define where the liability to pay tax arises (e.g. at the point of production or import, or alternatively at the point of retail sale?). This definition needs to be clear and unambiguous to ensure that each item sold is taxed and taxed only once. The taxes should apply equally to domestic production and imported goods to avoid distorting competition between domestic manufacturers and importers.

- Define the rate of tax or a procedure by which the rate of tax is to be determined.
- Include provisions for revising the tax in future years, in particular to take account of inflation.
- Define the responsibilities of taxpayers to provide required information for the administration of the tax (e.g. to register as producers or importers of the commodity subject to the tax, to provide a statement of the quantity produced or imported in the relevant period, to give access to other information that may be requested to verify the accuracy of this statement).
- Definition the time period over which the tax is assessed (monthly, quarterly or annual production and imports), and associated deadlines for filing required information and for making payments.
- Define the powers for investigation of tax evasion and penalties for failure to supply information or providing false or inaccurate information.

Implementation and monitoring

- Before introduction, develop a public communication strategy to explain the purpose and merits of the tax to address concerns that industry and households may have about the impact of the additional tax burden.
- Once the tax is operational, ensure that the effectiveness of its administration is regularly reviewed and any necessary improvements made.
- Put in place arrangements to ensure that tax rates are annually updated in line with inflation, to avoid the erosion of environmental effectiveness.

2. Deposit-refund systems

Key initial policy decisions

- Identify clearly the reason for introducing a DRS, bearing in mind the significant costs that DRS can impose on both producers and consumers.
- Decide whether to impose obligations on each producer to operate a DRS for their products or to establish a common industry-wide DRS covering all producers (a requirement for each firm to operate its own DRS can place a heavy burden on smaller producers).

Key legislative provisions

- Define the scope of the DRS so that it is clear which products are covered and which firms are required to participate in the scheme. To avoid distortion of competition, the scheme should apply equally to domestic producers and importers.
- Specify the deposit rate to be charged on each product, or setting up a procedure by which the deposit rates are to be determined and updated annually in line with inflation.
- For an industry-wide scheme, establish a public or an industry-run agency responsible for levying deposits, coordinating collection arrangements and

making refunds. Specify how the operating costs of the agency will be covered – through a levy per unit sold on all producers and importers, or through a financial allocation from the public budget.

- Require retail outlets to collect all items covered by the scheme and not just those that they have sold (some exemption from this obligation might be appropriate for small retailers).
- Require the agency to establish arrangements to reimburse retailers – regularly, fully and promptly – for the refunds they have paid out, basing the refunds on the quantity of items they have collected.
- Require the agency to make arrangements for recycling of collected items where these cannot be re-used by individual producers.
- Establish arrangements for covering the costs of the agency's operation and setting performance targets for the collection and recycling rates it should achieve, as well as respective annual reporting requirements.

Implementation and monitoring

- Develop and run a public information campaign to ensure that the public is aware of the DRS and the arrangements for product return.
- Monitor the agency's performance and investigate and address non-compliance by retail outlets.
- Update deposit rates periodically to avoid their erosion due to inflation.

3. Extended Producer Responsibility

Key initial policy decisions

- Identify clearly the purpose of introducing EPR in terms of separate management of wastes from the products selected for EPR. Shifting waste management costs from municipalities to firms is not a sufficient reason to justify the burden that EPR will impose on firms and consumers.
- Specify the scope of an EPR scheme in terms of the group of products to be covered (WEEE, packaging, end-of-life vehicles, etc.). If EPR schemes for more than one group of products are to be implemented, establish co-ordination arrangements for policy development, to ensure that, as far as practicable, they are established to a common design.

Key legislative provisions

- Set clear criteria to identify the firms to which the EPR obligations apply, with equal treatment of domestic producers and importers.
- Specify the constitution of the initial Producer Responsibility Organisation (PRO) through which firms can collectively discharge their obligations regarding the collection and recycling of the items covered by the scheme.
- Establish provisions to allow firms to opt out of the collective PRO and create their own collection arrangements, provided that they can demonstrate that they achieve the equivalent targets for collection and recycling rates.

- Specify the basis on which produces and importers are required to make annual contributions to the running costs of the PRO. This should be a clear and simple formula to divide up the total cost between participating firms in proportion to each firm's sales/imports of the products in question over the preceding year.
- Make a provision for the public budget to contribute an amount corresponding to the costs of handling the products of firms which have gone out of business.
- Specify how the collection and recycling performance targets for the PRO will be set and establish arrangements for annual financial audit and performance monitoring.
- Set the sanctions that will be applied to the PRO and its shareholder firms if it does not achieve its performance targets. These sanctions need to be at a level sufficient to ensure compliance and, therefore, should be set at a level that is likely to exceed the financial savings that firms might make through non-compliance.

Implementation and monitoring

- Develop and run a public information campaign to ensure that the public is aware of the arrangements for waste separation and product return.
- Set appropriate collection and recycling rate targets for the PRO (or each PRO, where more than one operate) before the start of the operating year.
- Require all PROs and any firms undertaking their own collection and recycling operations to report annually on the quantities of items collected and their subsequent re-use and recycling, their operating costs, income from sales of recycled materials, and the net operating cost to be financed by contributions from the participating firms. These statements should be subject to processes of both financial and environmental audit to verify their accuracy.
- After three years of operation, commission a study to assess the operation of the scheme, including the operating costs borne by firms and consumers and any adverse impacts on competition, and to make recommendations for any necessary changes.

ORGANISATION FOR ECONOMIC CO-OPERATION AND DEVELOPMENT

The OECD is a unique forum where governments work together to address the economic, social and environmental challenges of globalisation. The OECD is also at the forefront of efforts to understand and to help governments respond to new developments and concerns, such as corporate governance, the information economy and the challenges of an ageing population. The Organisation provides a setting where governments can compare policy experiences, seek answers to common problems, identify good practice and work to co-ordinate domestic and international policies.

The OECD member countries are: Australia, Austria, Belgium, Canada, Chile, the Czech Republic, Denmark, Estonia, Finland, France, Germany, Greece, Hungary, Iceland, Ireland, Israel, Italy, Japan, Korea, Luxembourg, Mexico, the Netherlands, New Zealand, Norway, Poland, Portugal, the Slovak Republic, Slovenia, Spain, Sweden, Switzerland, Turkey, the United Kingdom and the United States. The European Union takes part in the work of the OECD.

OECD Publishing disseminates widely the results of the Organisation's statistics gathering and research on economic, social and environmental issues, as well as the conventions, guidelines and standards agreed by its members.

OECD PUBLISHING, 2, rue André-Pascal, 75775 PARIS CEDEX 16
(97 2015 34 1 P) ISBN 978-92-64-24453-5 – 2015

www.ingramcontent.com/pod-product-compliance
Lightning Source LLC
LaVergne TN
LVHW081420110826
845149LV00010B/1810

* 9 7 8 9 2 6 4 2 4 4 5 3 5 *